THE VICTORIAN COUNTRY HOUSE

THE VICTORIAN COUNTRY HOUSE

FROM THE ARCHIVES OF COUNTRY LIFE

MICHAEL HALL

AURUM PRESS

First published in Great Britain 2009 by Aurum Press Limited
7 Greenland Street, London NW1 0ND
www.aurumpress.co.uk

A catalogue record for this book is available from the British Library
ISBN 978 1 84513 457 0

10 9 8 7 6 5 4 3 2 1
2013 2012 2011 2010 2009

Design by James Campus
Originated, printed and bound in Singapore by C S Graphics

Front endpaper: *Harlaxton Manor, Lincolnshire (1957)*
Rear endpaper: *Madresfield, Worcestershire (1980)*
Frontispiece: *The Front Hall, Arundel Castle, Sussex (1998)*

THE COUNTRY LIFE PICTURE LIBRARY

The *Country Life* Picture Library holds a complete set of prints made from its negatives, and a card index to the subjects, usually recording the name of the photographer and the date of the photographs catalogued, together with a separate index of photographers. It also holds a complete set of *Country Life* and various forms of published indices to the magazine.
The Library may be visited by appointment, and prints of any negatives it holds can be supplied by post.
For further information, please contact the Library Manager, Justin Hobson, at *Country Life*, Blue Fin Building, 110 Southwark Street, London SE1 0SU (*Tel:* 020 3148 4474).

ACKNOWLEDGEMENTS

It has been a great pleasure to work with the book's editor, Clare Howell, and designer, James Campus, both of whom have sustained this series of books from its inception. In *Country Life*'s Picture Library I have been guided at every stage by the Library Manager, Justin Hobson, and the Picture Researcher, Helen Carey. I have also been most grateful for the encouragement of the series editor, John Goodall. I would also like to thank Rosemary Hill for help with A. W. N. Pugin. Since so much of this book is based on work I did while employed by *Country Life* between 1989 and 2004, I would like also to acknowledge how much I owe to my former colleagues, in particular two successive editors, Jenny Greene and Clive Aslet, and my fellow members of the architectural department Jeremy Musson and Mary Miers. Although he retired the week before I started work at *Country Life*, I learned an immense amount from the magazine's last staff photographer, Alex Starkey, in many memorable conversations. I am also indebted to the first librarian of the picture library, Camilla Costello, and her team over the years, Olive Waller, Paula McGarry, Joyce Warren, Roger Ashe and Lulu. My greatest debt, however, is to the two colleagues with whom I shared an office in my days as an architectural writer, Giles Worsley and John Cornforth. They were more than happy to leave the Victorians to me and I shall always be grateful to them for that and very much else.

CONTENTS

*

'Between the villages of Hetton and Compton Last lies the extensive park of Hetton Abbey. This, formerly one of the notable houses of the county, was entirely rebuilt in 1864 in the Gothic style and is now devoid of interest. The grounds are open to the public daily until sunset and the house may be viewed on application by writing. It contains some good portraits and furniture. The terrace commands a fine view.'

Evelyn Waugh, *A Handful of Dust*, 1934

In June 1846, on holiday in Lausanne, Charles Dickens was introduced to Richard and Lavinia Watson, who instantly fell under his spell. He entertained them with readings from the early instalments of *Dombey and Son*, dedicated *David Copperfield* to them and visited their home, Rockingham Castle in Northamptonshire, where he produced and acted in plays in a theatre rigged up in the dining room. Dickens admired the Watsons' Liberal politics and enlightened custodianship of their house and estate, which was praised by Henry Hartshorne in his book *Rockingham Castle* (1852): 'The imagination strives to recall the glittering array of visor'd bowmen and feudal state, but these are supplanted by the smiling aspect of cottagers with their neatly cultivated gardens: a spacious school (itself no unworthy structure,) and the glittering spires thickly rising out of the vale of Welland, shew that an attention to the highest interest of the population has kept pace with their knowledge of an improved system of agriculture.'

It is one of the mysteries of Dickens's genius that this cheerful household and contented estate should, by his own admission, have become the principal model for the most celebrated country house in Victorian fiction, Chesney Wold, the melancholy Lincolnshire seat of Sir Leicester Dedlock in *Bleak House* (1852–53). The similarities are numerous: Rockingham's flag tower becomes the turret where the sinister lawyer Tulkinghorn sleeps, 'with a complaining flag-staff over his head'; Chesney Wold's Ghost's Walk is Rockingham's Yew Avenue; and Sir Leicester is glimpsed 'in a flush of crimson and gold, in the midst of the great drawing-room ... with broad strips of sunlight shining in, down the long perspective' – an apt description of Rockingham's long gallery. What is all the more surprising about the castle's transformation into fiction is that Dickens's imagination was stirred not by the impressive remains of Rockingham's thirteenth-century fortifications, or their conversion into an Elizabethan house, but by the improvements and alterations that the Watsons had themselves commissioned only three years before the book was written. Almost every architectural element of Chesney Wold echoes work carried out at Rockingham in 1849–51 by one of the most eminent country-house architects of early-Victorian times, Anthony Salvin. It was he who designed the flag tower, and added the keep tower at the end of the Yew Walk. He also extended the long gallery with a bay window that floods the room with light, a change that necessitated redecorating the room, with oak-grained woodwork, crimson silk-damask curtains, and green, white and gold wallpaper supplied by Cowtan & Sons in 1850 – a scheme that happily survives intact.

Rockingham's fictional transmutation mirrors the evolution of attitudes to Victorian country houses. Conceived by so many of their patrons as the backdrop to happy family life and rural improvement, for most of the twentieth century such buildings were regarded as the gloomy architectural relics of a feudal caste that had no place in modern life. Although within the past thirty years they have begun to be treated as proper objects for admiration, study and preservation, it is still difficult to disentangle the historical reality of country houses in the Victorian era from later attitudes to them.

That is a particular issue for a book on Victorian houses and interiors based on *Country Life*'s archive. In the years immediately after the magazine's foundation, in 1897, the ideals of architectural taste for which it was to stand for most of the twentieth century were only weakly evident in its pages, as its frequent articles on Victorian houses and gardens reveal. The photographs with which they are illustrated are significant historical documents for the study of new country houses, especially those that have been demolished. Then, from around 1910, the reaction against nineteenth-century design in all but its proto-Arts and Crafts manifestations becomes evident. From the First World War until the late 1950s, *Country Life*'s weekly articles on country houses largely avoided Victorian topics. This was not simply a matter of ignoring Victorian houses; alterations to earlier houses were disregarded, or, if unavoidable, deplored.

When Mark Girouard began to publish his series of articles on Victorian houses in the magazine, from the late 1950s onwards – the first scholarly examination anywhere of the subject – few great houses were still inhabited in a way that the Victorians would have recognized. A great number of Victorian houses had been converted to other uses, but even if they remained in family hands, their service wings had been converted or abandoned and the furnishings and decoration of their principal rooms had often been simplified or obliterated. The magazine

Above: *The long gallery at Rockingham Castle, Northamptonshire, an intact decorative scheme of 1850. The large bay window is an addition by Anthony Salvin.*

Left: *Edward Welby Pugin presents his design for the completion of Scarisbrick Hall, Lancashire, to Lady Scarisbrick, as depicted in a stained-glass window of 1865 by John Hardman at Scarisbrick. In the background is the house as Pugin intended it to look.*

has published articles on some astonishing survivals – Flintham, Brodsworth, Thoresby, Bishops Court, Stokesay, for example – but the frequent assumption that such houses are 'untouched' needs to be treated with care. The subject was set on a new scholarly basis by the publication in 1971 of Girouard's *The Victorian Country House*. By the time that a second, enlarged edition came out, in 1979, it was clear that the subject was popular. By the late 1980s, the magazine was recording the restoration of Victorian houses and interiors, often by the National Trust but also, with increasing frequency, by private owners, as at Rockingham, where in 1979–80 Michael Saunders-Watson had the long gallery's furnishings conserved. But whether these houses were photographed in their decline or in their renaissance, the fact remains that the great majority of *Country Life*'s photographs of nineteenth-century houses and interiors are in part documents of what the twentieth century has done to them.

Despite that major reservation, the archive is an almost inexhaustible resource for the study of Victorian houses. It is especially valuable for its breadth of focus. Virtually all books dealing with Victorian country houses confine themselves to new houses, yet the *Country Life* archive encompasses alterations to older houses, allowing us to study not simply the Victorian country house but also the country house in the

Top: *Osborne House, Queen Victoria and Prince Albert's home on the Isle of Wight. In the foreground is the pavilion wing, which contains the private apartments, completed in 1846; in the distance are the Household Wing and the 107-foot high flag tower.*

Above: *The picture gallery at Locko Park, Derbyshire, designed in 1861: an Italianate interior for the display of early Italian Old Masters – a combination made fashionable by Osborne.*

Victorian era, an approach that recognizes that every country-house architect and interior decorator of the time worked on both old and new houses. Secondly, most studies of Victorian country houses confine themselves to the strict definition of the subject – houses at the centre of a traditional landed estate. That makes it rather too easy to treat Victorian country houses as coterminous with a history of the aristocracy or the landed classes in the nineteenth century. *Country Life*'s definition of the subject, however, is based on the idea of a country house as a building type: in other words, it treats any architecturally ambitious house in the country as a country house. This is especially important in the nineteenth century, when for the first time large houses were built without estates or with estates so small that they could never even theoretically have provided an income to support them. A history of Victorian country houses must encompass not only landed houses, but also houses that look like them; the Victorian country house was in essence a matter of image as well as economics.

⚜ ⚜ ⚜

Almost everything that it is now regarded as distinctive about the Victorian country house was in place before Victoria ascended the throne in 1837. As John Martin Robinson has written in the preceding title in this series, *The Regency Country House*, 'The English country house as we know it – the centre of a self-contained estate and the setting for house parties – is essentially a product of the Regency era.' The concept of an estate as a unified area consolidated in single ownership and centred on a country house, complete with lodges, estate villages and tenant farms under the supervision of an agent, was a creation of the late eighteenth and early nineteenth centuries. The notion of a great aristocrat's feudal domain is so potent that it is easy to assume that, for example, the 1st Duke of Westminster, whose family had been seated at Eaton in Cheshire since the fifteenth century, was simply continuing traditions set by his ancestors in the programme of estate improvements that he began in the 1870s. In fact, before 1811, as Dr Robinson points out, the land around Eaton Hall was owned by fourteen proprietors, whom the Grosvenors had to buy out.

If the idea of an estate as understood by the Victorians was largely a modern creation, then so also to a large extent was the country house. In the mid-eighteenth century the planning of great houses as sequences of formal apartments, a tradition that goes back to the Middle Ages, was definitively abandoned in favour of a loose, accretive arrangement of reception rooms – a drawing room and dining room, and usually a library at the very least – around a hall. Many of the features thought of as distinctively Victorian – from service wings and large conservatories to plate-glass windows, lavish upholstery, fitted carpets, central heating, plumbed-in baths and WCs – were all available to the patrons and architects of Regency houses.

The social life for which Victorian houses were designed also continued the traditions laid down in the previous generation. Balls and other parties were a metropolitan fashion, which had spread widely to country houses by 1800. By the early nineteenth century, long house parties, which had been the customary form of country-house entertaining, had been supplemented by 'Saturday to Monday' parties, weekend visits that were facilitated by greatly improved road transport. Thanks to the railway, this form of entertaining became the norm for Victorian country houses. Sport, always at the heart of the attraction of country-house life, had largely been equestrian until the early nineteenth century, when the invention of more reliable forms of gun, and the introduction of driven game with beaters, laid the foundation of the shooting parties that gave Victorian country houses a large part of their *raison d'être* in the autumn and winter.

In what ways, therefore, was the Victorian country house distinctive? One evident change followed the death of George IV in 1830. From that point, the royal family never again led fashion in the way that the King, as Prince Regent, had established: there was no replacement for his enthusiasm for artistic innovation and gorgeous display, which had set the fast pace of Regency taste. Yet Victoria and Albert undoubtedly had an influence on country houses. The change in tone in aristocratic life that was so marked by the 1840s – away from private indulgence towards public respectability – had many causes, most importantly the influence of the Evangelical religious revival and the change in the political balance of power after the Great Reform Act of 1832. But a significant influence was the tone of the Court, now the setting for a contented family life, which was in sharp contrast to George IV's domestic circumstances. The Victorian emphasis on country houses as above all family homes would probably not have resounded with such force throughout the century without a royal model.

Although neither Albert nor Victoria has a reputation as a pioneer in terms of architectural patronage, the two houses that they jointly created, Osborne House on the Isle of Wight, built in 1845–48, and Balmoral in Aberdeenshire, completed in 1856, were significantly influential. The latter helped to popularize the Victorian cult of the Highlands and gave a fillip to the baronial revival in architecture. Osborne, picturesquely Italianate in its use of stucco-like render, belvedere towers and loggias, has more complex origins. It may owe a debt to Charles Barry's use of the style, most famously at Trentham in Staffordshire, home of Victoria's close friend Harriet, Duchess of Sutherland. It seems possible that it was only Prince Albert's suspicion of Barry – 'every step Sir Charles takes requires careful watching', he remarked in 1853 – that led to a builder, Thomas Cubitt, rather than a professional architect, being chosen to design the house. It may be, however, simply that Albert wanted to have as free a hand as possible in the attention he paid to to every detail of its construction. Osborne's magnificent silhouette, so clearly visible from the Solent, evokes not only Barry but also the Italianate fashions in contemporary German architecture that Albert would have known, such as Ludwig Persius's Orangery Palace at Potsdam, Osborne's exact contemporary.

That Italo-Germanic flavour extends to the interior, where the imagination has to strip away the accretions made in Victoria's widowhood to recover the spareness and Cinquecento elegance that these rooms originally possessed. Albert admired Germany's Nazarene painters, whose works he collected, and he commissioned William Dyce, a painter deeply influenced by the Nazarenes, to provide a fresco – *Neptune Entrusting the Command of the Sea to Britannia* – for the head of the staircase. This is surrounded by painted decoration of *grottesche* in the manner of Raphael's Vatican *loggie*, almost certainly by Albert's principal artistic adviser, Ludwig Gruner. This taste for the Italian Renaissance was reflected in Albert's picture collecting: his dressing room contained a group of paintings by, or attributed to, Gozzoli, Verrocchio and Cima. Architecturally, Osborne had direct progeny in English country houses – Mark Girouard traces a family tree leading from Samuel Daukes's Abberley Hall, Worcestershire (1845) to John Giles's Highfield in Gloucestershire of around 1869 – but almost any Classical Victorian mansion has echoes of the house: Brodsworth's drawing room, for example, is strikingly similar to Osborne's columned reception rooms. More subtly, the taste for Italianate painted decoration and early Italian pictures evident in several mid-century houses suggests congruity with Osborne if not actual influence: for example, William Drury-Lowe's collecting of early Italian pictures probably owes nothing to Albert's direct example, but when he inherited Locko Park in Derbyshire in 1849, he added a belvedere tower and hired a painter from Florence to execute Italianate decorative schemes – both additions that immediately evoke Osborne. Indeed, a taste for Italian interiors is one of the most persistent themes in country houses right through the century, encompassing, for example, the 3rd Marquess of Bath's interiors at Longleat in the 1870s and Viscount Windsor's new Hewell Grange in the 1880s.

Neither Albert nor Victoria showed any significant architectural interest in the Gothic Revival, in part, no doubt, because of the Queen's well-recorded dislike for the High Church. A taste for Gothic was already spectacularly evident in the Regency, most notably in William Porden's stupendous Gothic rebuilding of Eaton Hall for the 2nd Earl Grosvenor, James Wyatt's Ashridge for the 7th Earl of Bridgewater and two interiors in the Prince of Wales's Carlton House in London – John Nash's Gothic drawing room and Thomas Hopper's conservatory, modelled on Henry VII's Chapel at Westminster Abbey. Indeed, for all that the Gothic Revival is inextricably associated with the Victorians, very few Victorian patrons of Gothic architecture accomplished anything on quite the scale of those Regency palaces.

To the taste for Gothic should be added an interest in the revival and redecoration of castles, a fashion pioneered by the 1st Duke of Northumberland at Alnwick Castle in the mid-eighteenth century and developed on an impressive scale in the Regency by the 5th Duke of Rutland at Belvoir and George IV at Windsor. This tradition was continued vigorously throughout the nineteenth century: in the period between the 2nd Duke of Cleveland's remodelling of Raby Castle in the 1840s and the 15th Duke of Norfolk's rebuilding of Arundel Castle's western range, completed in 1901, the Victorian aristocracy staged a spectacular finale to the thousand-year association of castles with landed power. The use of medieval styles – which in the Regency included 'Saxon', or as we should say Norman – seemed peculiarly suitable for noblemen, who liked to imply that most traced their titles to the Middle Ages (something that was actually extremely rare in England). In the early nineteenth century the combination of medieval-revival architecture with eighteenth-century French furnishings, including *boiseries*, as at Belvoir Castle and Windsor, also proclaimed the continuity in England of the monarchical and aristocratic traditions severed in France – but within a framework of ancient English liberty.

As the nineteenth century progressed, these two traditions – medievalism and the art of the *ancien règime* – largely went their separate ways. A taste for French interiors persisted until the end of the nineteenth century, in part thanks to the appetite for French decorative arts associated with the Rothschilds and their competitors in the salerooms, such as the 4th Marquess of Hertford and 1st Earl of Dudley, and also because Rococo was felt to be a style peculiarly appropriate for interiors allocated to the female sphere, such as bedrooms and, most importantly, drawing rooms. '*Tous les Louis*' interiors (an eclectic mix of eighteenth-century French styles) were commonplace by the 1840s in Elizabethan or Jacobean Revival houses as well as Classical ones, a tradition which persisted to the end of the century. Gothic, by contrast,

Above: *A design for the great hall at Scarisbrick Hall, Lancashire, drawn by A. W. N. Pugin in about 1840.*

Right: *The garden front of Kelham Hall, Nottinghamshire, designed by George Gilbert Scott in 1858. In the distance is the service wing of 1844–46 by Anthony Salvin, which survived the 1856 fire that destroyed the main house.*

became an exclusive style. Architects, thanks largely to the ardent propaganda of A. W. N. Pugin, wanted Gothic to be a style for all purposes, including interior design. In one sense Pugin broke Gothic's association with the aristocracy by insisting that it was suitable for all types of house, however modest. In other ways, he reinforced it by seeking to create houses for noblemen that were much closer to medieval originals. The key element in this was the revival of the great hall. Pugin was not responsible for its reintroduction into English domestic architecture – that honour probably goes to Thomas Rickman and John Slater when they opened up the subdivided great hall at Scarisbrick Hall, Lancashire, during their 1812–16 remodelling of the house – but it was Pugin who argued that such interiors were not just an antiquarian pleasure: they were a social necessity.

Pugin's most vivid statement of the ideal that the great hall represented – an ideal with which a medieval nobleman would undoubtedly have concurred – was set out in 1841 in his *True Principles of Pointed or Christian Architecture*: 'the almost constant residence of the ancient gentry on their estates rendered it indispensable for them to have mansions where they might exercise their rights of hospitality to their fullest extent. They did not confine their guests, as at present, to a few fashionables who condescend to pass away a few days occasionally in a country house; but under the oaken rafters of their capacious halls the lords of the manor used to assemble all their friends and tenants at those successive periods when the church bids all her children rejoice, while humbler guests partook of their share of bounty dealt to them by the hand of the almoner beneath the groined entrance of the gatehouse.' To some degree this vision of social harmony was echoed in practice, in, for example, the guest hall at Alnwick or the great hall at Thoresby, both designed by Anthony Salvin in part for the annual entertainments of tenants, or for festivities to celebrate, for example, a successful election or an heir's coming-of-age.

Not all architects were entirely comfortable with this exclusively feudal vision. Although in his *Remarks on Secular and Domestic Architecture Present and Future* (1857), a plea for the universal use of Gothic, George Gilbert Scott reiterates many of Pugin's arguments about great halls, he adds, 'I remember being once at the house of a nobleman on an occasion when, had he not possessed a great hall, it would have been next to impossible to have entertained the company invited, though the circumstances were such as rendered it quite necessary to invite them, and that without limitation of numbers. Such occasions are decidedly on the increase. Large assemblies are called together by meetings of scientific societies, agricultural meetings, consecrations

and re-openings of churches, and many other causes which render this enlarged hospitality on the part of the great man of the neighbourhood both desirable and practically of frequent occurrence.' The idea that a great hall could serve as a committee room or lecture hall is consistent with Scott's belief that the style was adaptable to all modern needs, a fundamental tenet amongst Gothic architects by the 1850s.

Moreover, Scott, like Pugin towards the end of his life, and like such leading designers as William Butterfield, G. E. Street and William White, came to believe that what was needed was not the revival of Gothic but its development into a modern style. In part this was to be accomplished by a broader range of sources for a new stylistic synthesis, including most importantly foreign forms of Gothic, and secondly by making full use of new or newly available materials, such as machine-polished granite, an innovation of the 1840s, encaustic tiles and native as well as imported marbles. The result of such ideals can be seen in Scott's country houses, most completely perhaps at Kelham Hall in Nottinghamshire, designed in 1858 for John Henry Manners-Sutton. Impressive although Kelham is – even though it was never completed – it reveals the difficulties that architects faced in manipulating developed Gothic into forms consonant with domestic purposes. The style perhaps works better on a smaller scale, as at Butterfield's Milton Ernest and White's Bishops Court, but the Goths were not alone in finding it difficult to transform avant-garde architectural innovation from a small to a large scale.

Great halls had a practical purpose also in terms of planning, as they were useful circulation spaces in large buildings, as Thoresby in particular reveals. Even patrons for whom Gothic was out of the question for reasons of the style's Christian associations could see their value. The result was a fashion for large, often top-lit halls evident in the 1850s, most famously the great central living hall or saloon at Mentmore Towers, Buckinghamshire, designed for Baron Mayer de Rothschild by G. H. Stokes and Joseph Paxton in 1850. The disadvantage of such large spaces is that even with central heating they are likely to be draughty. For that reason, when Mayer de Rothschild's nephew Ferdinand commissioned Waddesdon Manor in 1874 he instructed his architect, Gabriel-Hippolyte Destailleur, that no such hall was to be provided. However, within only a couple of years of the house's completion, he could see that he had sacrificed too much, as there was no room sufficiently large for all his guests to congregate in, and so Destailleur returned to add a large morning room.

Scott's *Remarks* was no doubt intended in part to attract clients, and it may well have succeeded. Scott had given the lectures on which the book is based in Newark in 1855, which may explain how he came to Manners-Sutton's notice as a potential architect for nearby Kelham. Yet, judged purely as self-advertisement, *Remarks* is modest in comparison with some of the books and manuals on country-house design, which proliferated in the nineteenth century. This partly reflects a phenomenon that was still new at the beginning of Victoria's reign: the professionalization of architecture. The first president of the Institute of British Architects, founded in 1834, was Earl de Grey, who was probably the last amateur architect to design a country house on a grand scale, Wrest Park, completed in 1839 – although of course he employed a professional clerk-of-works to supervise its construction. From then on, the employment of an architect was *de rigueur*. Even a landowner with a sustained passion for architecture, such as Roland Egerton-Warburton, who commissioned a new house, Arley Hall in Cheshire, in 1832 and rebuilt many of the estate cottages, was contemptuous of amateur designers. In a long poem in rhyming couplets, *A Looking Glass for Landlords* (1875), he wrote, 'Who thinks himself he can his house erect/ Employs a noodle for an architect;/ Choose your own site, adapt what style you will,/ Then counsel take with one of taste and will.'

When selecting an architect, patrons no doubt largely relied on private recommendation – numerous architects had circles of clients linked by family or political associations – but it was possible for a designer to come to the eye of a client through a book, especially perhaps when that patron did not come from a traditional landowning background. When in 1868 the proprietor of *The Times*, John Walter, gave a speech to the workmen who were building his new country house, Bear Wood in Berkshire, he revealed that he had chosen his architect, Robert Kerr, on the basis of Kerr's book *The Gentleman's House; Or How to Plan English Residences, from the Parsonage to the Palace with Tables of Accommodation and Cost, and a Series of Selected Plans*, published in 1864. Kerr's book is the best known Victorian manual of domestic design, an exhaustive and faintly pompous guide to every element of planning and domestic technology, from general principles ('the character of a gentleman-like residence is not a matter of magnitude or of costliness, but of design, – and chiefly of plan') to the details of fitting out a fish-larder ('a broad slate or marble table all round, and a few hooks above').

Left: *Mentmore Towers, Buckinghamshire, designed for Baron Mayer de Rothschild in 1850 by G. H. Stokes and Joseph Paxton. The very large service court is visible on the right.*

Above right: *Alupka, on the Black Sea coast in the Crimea, designed for Count Mikhail Vorontsov by Edward Blore and built in the 1840s. Vorontsov had close links with England: his sister Catherine was married to the 11th Earl of Pembroke.*

One reason for a client deferring to a professional architect was the ever-increasing importance of domestic technology, particularly plumbing, central heating, ventilation and draught proofing. Although it is not hard to find unfavourable comments about the chilly temperatures in country houses from visiting Americans, unused to life in historic buildings, the emphasis on comfort and indeed luxury that had been so evident in country-house design in Regency times was sustained throughout Victoria's reign, as most visitors recognized. The best known – and one of the best informed – account of English country-house design was published by the former German cultural attaché Hermann Muthesius in 1904. His book, *Das Englische Haus*, lays consistent stress on the technological superiority of English domestic architecture over its European counterparts. Although he was writing when the design of English houses was undergoing a period of exceptional creativity, international admiration for the country's tradition of country-house life goes back to the early nineteenth century. This resulted in a number of English architects designing houses for foreign clients. An early example is Alupka on the Crimea's Black Sea coast, designed by Edward Blore, one of the most prolific of early-Victorian country-house architects, for Count Mikhail Vorontsov. Completed in the mid-1840s, it is externally a remarkable synthesis of Jacobean and Islamic styles; internally, its library, modelled on Walter Scott's Abbotsford, oak-panelled dining room and billiard room would not look out of place in the Scottish borders. The same could be said for E. B. Lamb's Elizabethan interiors at Schloss Hrádek in the Czech Republic, installed in the 1850s. Even a relatively minor architect, such as John Norton, designer of Tyntesfield, was responsible for country houses in Lithuania and Estonia.

One major development in Victoria's reign was the replacement of the traditional method of building country houses, in which a clerk-of-works, usually a member of the estate staff, directly employed the builders and other craftsmen, in favour of the customary commercial

Right: *The Octagon Drawing Room, Raby Castle, Co. Durham, decorated and furnished in 1848 by George Morant, working under the direction of William Burn for the 2nd Duke of Cleveland.*

Below: *The State Drawing Room, Knebworth House, Hertfordshire, decorated and furnished in 1844 for Sir Edward Bulwer Lytton by Crace & Son.*

practice of contracting out the work to a firm of builders. Clients recommended not only architects but also builders to each other: for example, after working on Mentmore Towers, the London-based firm of George Myers was employed by numerous other members of the Rothschild family. By the mid-century a few metropolitan firms dominated the trade: William Cubitt & Sons built both Osborne and Tyntesfield and Edward Conder was responsible for both Waddesdon Manor and Stokesay Court – 'I have never met a more trustworthy man of business', wrote Ferdinand Rothschild, and had an inscription recording Conder's role carved on the east front of Waddesdon. But a few country houses continued to be built by the old method. Although the sheer number of workmen involved (380 men were on site at Bear Wood in 1868) makes evident the advantage of using a contractor, some patrons, such as Viscount Windsor at Hewell Grange in the 1880s, preferred using direct labour as it offered the flexibility to make changes as work progressed; he seems not to have minded that the house as a result took seven years to build.

The architect's replacement of the amateur in country-house design was accompanied by the rise of another, much less well-studied, profession, that of the upholsterer, who furnished and decorated houses, and – often in total independence from the architect – could be responsible for complete schemes of interior design which went far beyond the provision of carpets and curtains. All the big specialist firms could provide virtually everything needed to equip a country house on the largest scale. At Stokesay Court, for example, the architect's involvement went no further than designing the panelling and chimneypieces. Everything else, from bell pulls to picture frames, came from Hampton & Sons in Pall Mall, who also wallpapered and painted the rooms. The best known of these firms is Crace & Son, based in Wigmore Street. Like many of the large Victorian upholstery firms, it had its roots in the late eighteenth century and Regency: founded in 1768, it came to prominence working for the Prince Regent at Brighton and for Queen Victoria at Windsor.

An early and characteristic example of the way such a firm could create an entire new look for a house is J. G. Crace's decoration of Knebworth House in Hertfordshire, after it was inherited by the immensely popular novelist Sir Edward Bulwer Lytton in 1843. The richly polychromatic and heraldic decoration provided by Crace took its cue from Lytton's romantic passion for his medieval ancestry in a remarkable fusion of decorative painting, textiles, stained glass and new Gothic furniture. Some details may reflect the influence of A. W. N. Pugin, whom Crace had met by the time work began. Pugin and Crace worked together on numerous occasions, most notably in the Palace of Westminster, and Crace continued to supply Gothic interiors using designs by Pugin or in a deluxe version of his style for many years after the architect's death in 1852. Crace, however, did not share Pugin's exclusive emphasis on Gothic, and the firm's finest surviving country-house interiors are the sumptuous Italian Renaissance state rooms at Longleat, designed in the 1870s by J. G. Crace's son, John Dibblee Crace, for the 4th Marquess of Bath.

Schemes such as those at Knebworth and Longleat, which have escaped the twentieth-century reaction against Victorian design, reveal the work of interior decorators of the calibre of Crace to have been extraordinarily impressive in execution as well as design. Since so many Victorian country houses have passed out of domestic use, it is essential to visit such rooms to understand why contemporaries were so impressed by the luxury and splendour of country-house life in the nineteenth century. Indeed, it was sometimes felt that the modern emphasis on grandeur and comfort was inappropriate for ancient buildings. In its description of medieval Raby Castle, Co. Durham, expensively refurnished for the 2nd Duke of Cleveland in the 1840s, Murray's 1873 *Handbook for Durham and Northumberland* icily quoted the antiquary William Howitt: 'when we step in and find ourselves at once in modern drawing rooms, with silken couches and gilt cornice ... we forget that we are at Raby, the castle of the victors of Neville's Cross, and of Joan, the daughter of John of Gaunt, and feel that we are only in the saloons of the modern Duke of Cleveland.' Luckily, one of the interiors at Raby created by the eminent London decorators George Morant under the direction of William Burn, the Octagon Drawing Room, survives intact in all its colourful glamour.

The best known decorators, such as Crace, whose standard of design was comparable with the finest that contemporary architects could offer, were considered expensive, as William Gibbs was rather shocked to discover when he received the bill for Crace's work at Tyntesfield. Other, more commercial firms, such as Maple & Co. of Tottenham Court Road, now seem to us astonishingly cheap, especially in comparison with building costs. At Stokesay Court, for example, Allcroft paid Hampton's only £1,109 for the fitting-out of a house that cost £82,233 to build. Yet he paid £3,526 to equip the house with electricity, a sum that did not include the building of an engine house. This makes plain how expensive technology was in comparison with traditional skills, a complete inversion of twenty-first century economics. At Arundel Castle, for example, the pre-eminent architectural sculptor Thomas Earp charged £150 for carving the enormous chimneypiece in the drawing room, whereas the provision of electricity cost £28,652.

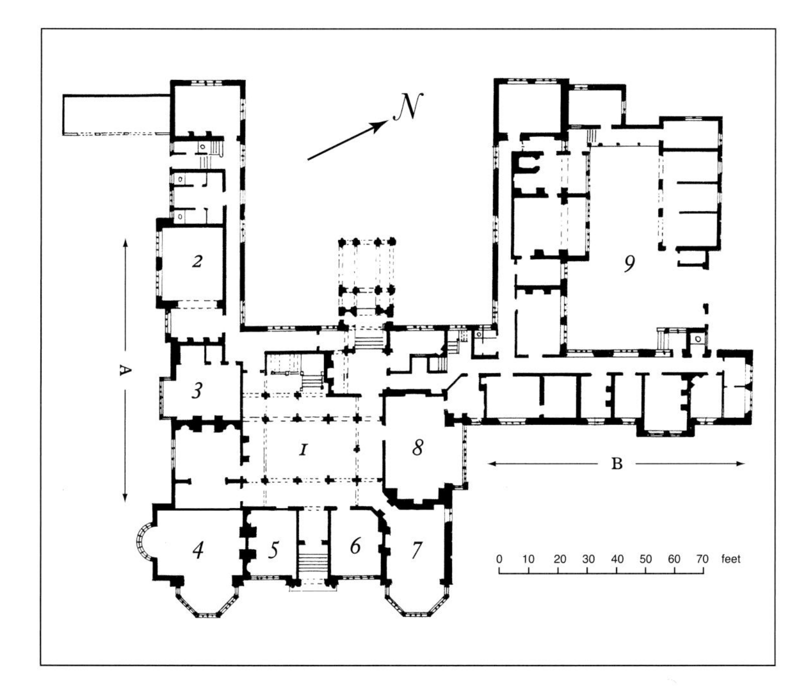

Top: *The Young Ladies' Boudoir, Stokesay Court, Shropshire. This first-floor sitting room was provided for female guests.*

Above: *Ground-floor plan of Stokesay Court, Shropshire.* A: *The Gentleman's Wing;* B: *The Ladies' Wing. 1: The hall; 2: The billiard room; 3: The business room; 4: The drawing room; 5: The portrait parlour; 6: The morning room; 7: The library; 8: The dining room; 9: The service court.*

Left: *Bear Wood, Berkshire, designed in 1864. Its architect, Robert Kerr, won the commission on the strength of his popular manual of domestic design,* The Gentleman's House *(1864).*

As Kerr emphasized, what clients wanted more even than technology or splendid decoration was a convenient plan, and leading country-house architects especially prided themselves on their skill in devising them. Realizing how such a reputation lay at the foundation of his enormous success in gaining country-house commissions, Burn would never allow his plans to be published: when he discovered that Kerr had obtained a plan for one of his houses from one of his assistants for publication in *The Gentleman's House* he refused permission for it to appear, leaving Kerr to publish in its place a 'design on the modern Scotch model' of his own (the words 'after the late Mr. Burn' were added in subsequent editions).

Two factors in particular governed the plan of Victorian houses, privacy and propriety, and both to some degree mark elaborations of earlier norms. A consistent theme in the planning of great houses since the early Middle Ages had been the provision of privacy for a house's owners by creating accommodation that was clearly separate from that of visitors and servants. This was achieved in two ways, firstly by providing a private domestic wing, already commonplace by the early Victorian period; in the largest establishments, such as Eaton Hall, this could in effect become a separate house. Such a wing allowed the routines of family life, most notably the care of children, to be separated from a house's function as a place of entertainment; Kerr recommended also that it include a gentleman's sitting room for the transaction of estate business. Secondly, and more significantly, servants were completely segregated from the family household into service wings. Although already a feature of Regency houses, they grew dramatically in size, and by the mid-nineteenth century were frequently as large or larger in plan than the main body of the house. The positioning of service quarters in a basement, common enough at the beginning of the century, was almost entirely discarded by the early part of Victoria's reign. Kerr, writing that basement offices are 'scarcely ever to be recommended', gives a plan showing how, in the 1860s, T. H. Wyatt added service accommodation to Giacomo Leoni's Palladian Lathom Hall, Lancashire, in order to remove the kitchen and its ancillary services from the main body of the house.

Such changes reinforced the privacy of the owner and his family and removed such unwanted elements as cooking smells from a house; they also provided more spacious and better-lit accommodation for servants, something that most country-house owners came to regard as an important responsibility. There is evidence that some took a close interest in the design of service accommodation. When Burn was working on the designs for Sandon Hall in the 1850s he had to fend off amendments to the proposed arrangement of the service quarters by his (admittedly unusually interfering) clients, the Earl and Countess of Harrowby. Lady Harrowby's proposed 'plate scullery' was dismissed by Burn as 'utterly useless' and he brushed aside the request for a flour room: 'a binn in the Bake house is all that is necessary, and as much as nine out of ten Private bakehouses ever have'. Such interventions by his clients suggest almost that ambitious service wings were something of a status symbol, a suspicion reinforced by the pride with which the Harrowbys showed theirs off to visitors: in 1859 Cecylia Dzialynska recorded the tour that they gave her: 'Separate rooms for cleaning lamps, separate for cleaning shoes, another only for silver, lined by green felt covered shelves behind the matching curtains, further on a place for washing china, and still further for ceramics, and then again a little room for all maids' paraphernalia i.e. all brooms, rugs, pails, dusters, everything so clean and neatly arranged it's a pleasure.'

Such provision, which was by no means unusual, was not a consequence of an increased number of servants. Throughout the century, the maximum size of domestic staff rarely rose above thirty, the number accommodated in one of the grandest of all Victorian houses, Eaton Hall. Why, therefore, did service wings grow so much? The mystery is deepened by Muthesius's assertion that it was a peculiarly English phenomenon: 'every size of house in England contains between twice and four times as many domestic rooms as the continental house.' Despite the fact that large service wings are such a familiar part of the modern image of a Victorian country house, surprisingly little attention has been paid to them by social historians, a reflection in part of gaps in the documentary sources – servants are largely silent witnesses to country-house life for most of the nineteenth century – and a neglect of domestic service by historians in favour of studying the supposedly more independent lives of workers in industry. Yet service in a large house was relatively unusual for working-class men and virtually unique for working-class women in providing a well-developed career ladder, and domestic staff often moved between households in pursuit of higher status or better pay and perquisites. It is possible therefore, although the subject certainly needs more investigation, that the elaboration of Victorian service wings was driven by servants' demand for not only comfort and convenience but also, by the provision of dedicated rooms for particular activities and occupations, recognition of their place in a well-defined domestic hierarchy.

Propriety, another guiding principle of the planning of country houses, affected both the main body of the house and the service wing, and in particular the creation of distinct and well-separated accommodation for men and women. The Victorian country house developed a geography of gender to a degree that had not previously existed, with the provision of social spaces that were clearly defined as masculine or feminine. Drawing rooms and morning rooms were conceived of as female, libraries as masculine – Kerr even describes the library as 'primarily a sort of Morning-room for gentlemen rather than anything else', a statement that needs to be set against Muthesius's rather surprising claim that 'large collection of books are on the whole much more common in English houses than in German.' Yet all these rooms were used to some degree by both sexes. That was not the case with the smoking room – virtually unknown at the start of Victoria's reign, ubiquitous at its end – which were exclusively male domains; the only door in the private apartments at Osborne to bear the monogram 'A' rather than an entwined 'V' and 'A' was that of the smoking room. Such rooms were often incorporated into suites for men, with gun rooms and billiard rooms. In compensation, women increasingly had rooms set aside for their exclusive use, often close to the bedrooms: at Stokesay Court, for example, there was a 'Young Ladies' Boudoir' on the first floor, furnished with white woodwork imitating Chippendale and upholstered in pink silk. Stokesay's plan takes to an extreme what had become a customary division of the genders. The west side of the main house is occupied by a Gentleman's Wing, containing the billiard room, card room and business room, with bachelors' bedrooms above; the ladies bedrooms are as far away as possible, in the wing that forms the south side of the service courtyard. This plan had practical disadvantages – as the historian Jill Franklin points out, 'all bedroom slops from the gentleman's wing must have passed through the hall.'

This division of genders reinforces curiosity about how much influence women had on country-house design. Again this is a subject that deserves greater investigation, but it is clear that independent female patrons, such as Lady Scarisbrick at Scarisbrick Hall, were very rare. However, there is plenty of evidence of husbands consulting their wives – at Sandon, for example, the Countess of Harrowby seems to have been as fully involved in discussions with Burn as her husband and eldest son. At Stokesay, Allcroft's wife, Mary, intervened during the building of the house with occasional wry asperity. When she discovered that the baths her husband had authorized to be installed were too small and could not be changed without considerable expense, she demonstrated her point by having a builder climb into one of the baths so that she could measure the likely height of the water: 'it is such

Above: *The entrance lodge at Kinmel Park, Denbighshire, designed by William Eden Nesfield in 1868.*

Right: *The garden front of Leyswood, Groombridge, Sussex, designed by Richard Norman Shaw and built in 1868–69. This plate from* The Building News *(1871) is taken from an 1870 drawing by Shaw. It demonstrates how he was able to preserve the drama and picturesque variety of Gothic design in his new and influential 'Old English' idiom. The patron, James Savill, was a cousin of Shaw and a director of the Shaw Savill shipping company.*

a fuss altering these things, I wish you would sometimes listen to me', she wrote to her husband. However, the influence of women on the design of the country houses in which they were to live may well be summarized in a remark by the wife of Lord Coleridge, who commissioned Butterfield's rebuilding of Chanter's House: 'my husband tells me he worships the ground I tread on', she once told a friend, 'but I am never allowed to choose the carpets.'

The provision of gun rooms, smoking rooms and billiard rooms as well as such amenities as conservatories or picture galleries, and, in particular, gardens, emphasizes also that country houses were designed in large part for pleasure and entertainment. At Waddesdon Manor, for example, inspection of the house's magnificent collections of paintings, porcelain and furniture was an almost insignificant element in the delights laid on by Ferdinand Rothschild for his summer house parties: visitors were able to take tours of the enormous glass houses, visit the menagerie and aviary, sample cream in the model dairy, inspect the stables and travel in a miniature steam launch along the River Thame for tea at his sister Alice's house at Eythrope. Although at Waddesdon such pleasures were designed with a Rothschild lavishness and perfectionism, a version of such pastimes was available in most country houses. They are a reminder that a substantial motive for wishing to acquire a country house was the enjoyment they offered as well as the status and power they provided, or at least symbolized. Indeed, to partake regularly in shooting, the most popular sport of the late-nineteenth-century upper classes, it was almost essential to own land, as very few shoots were let before the 1890s.

This helps to explain why country houses remained so popular throughout the nineteenth century, a fact that is often obscured by the undoubted decline of the value of land both financially and symbolically from the 1870s onwards. The agricultural depression, which was at its most severe from the late 1870s to the late 1890s, caused largely by the import of cheap grain from North America, badly affected the agricultural revenues of most large estate owners, especially in the south and east of the country. It is not clear, however, that this had much direct influence on the creation of new houses. Already by the early nineteenth century very few houses were being built on the back of agricultural revenues; even in the so-called 'golden age' of British agriculture, from the 1840s to 1870s, land was never especially attractive judged purely as an investment. The Victorian country house, like its Regency predecessor, was largely built with the proceeds of industry, banking and urban rents, which makes the efforts of so many historians to distinguish between 'traditional' and 'nouveaux-riches' houses a fruitless exercise. Land was, however, attractive as an essential basis for political influence, the main reason why the Rothschilds, for example, invested so heavily in estate purchase in the 1840s. It was inconceivable for most of the nineteenth century that a politician could achieve the highest offices without a landed background, which is why in 1847 Benjamin Disraeli bought the Hughenden estate in Buckinghamshire.

Although it was not until 1908, with the election of H. H. Asquith, that a British prime minister possessed no country estate, the need for a politician to own land had long before that evaporated, thanks to the extension of the franchise and the steady – if in some ways surprisingly slow – ebbing of power from the aristocracy. After the general election of 1885 landowners were for the first time ever in a minority in the House of Commons. Added to that was a shift in popular opinion away from the traditional respect accorded to land, fomented from the 1880s onwards by a Liberal Party emphasis on land reform and campaigns for a land tax to achieve a more equable distribution of the nation's wealth. The tax was never introduced, but the minority Liberal government of 1892–95 did manage to impose the first effective death duties, designed, wrote Gladstone, to 'strike at the very heart of class-preference.' It is no wonder, therefore, that in Oscar Wilde's 1895 comedy *The Importance of Being Earnest* Lady Bracknell expresses the view, 'land has ceased to be either a profit or a pleasure. It gives one position, and prevents one from keeping it up.'

Yet although such attitudes undoubtedly affected attitudes to the desirability of country estates, they had very little direct impact on the desirability of country houses. Indeed, the last quarter of the nineteenth century witnessed a remarkable flowering of the form, even if the patrons who created them were no longer the traditional landed classes or even the newly wealthy investing in landed estates. This in part reflects the way that in the later nineteenth century taste was created largely by the middle classes. The late-Victorian country house has its origins in the 1860s, when most architects abandoned the belief that Gothic was a desirable style for domestic architecture. A leading country-house architect, George Devey, who was especially popular with Liberal landowners, including the Rothschilds, was among the first to experiment with styles drawn from vernacular precedent, with charming results in small buildings such as cottages and lodges. However, he found it difficult to translate this success into the large scale needed for country houses, a problem that even architects who worked with fluency in the new 'Queen Anne' and Aesthetic Movement styles did not always overcome. At Kinmel Park in Denbighshire, for example, remodelled by W. E. Nesfield in a free and aestheticized version of Wren's Classicism in 1871–74, the main house is outshone by the exquisite beauty of its lodge. The most successful

'Queen Anne' country houses, such as Ken Hill in Norfolk, designed by J. J. Stevenson in 1879–80, are moderate in size. Edward Green, its owner, conceived it essentially as a holiday house

The one architect who could move effortlessly from the smallest scale to the largest was Richard Norman Shaw. His creation in the 1860s – in collaboration with Nesfield, with whom he was in informal partnership at the outset of his career – of the 'Old English' style in such houses as Leyswood and Glen Andred in Surrey and Cragside in Northumberland, offered the first wholly convincing alternative to Gothic, that preserved the flexibility of planning and massing that had made Gothic appealing. It was thanks to Shaw, in such houses as Adcote in Shropshire (1878), that the great hall had a renaissance as a grand but comfortable living hall. The style owed a considerable debt to Philip Webb, but Shaw possessed a fluency in composition and a gift for planning that Webb lacked. Shaw's success was grounded in part on his thorough training in the principles of country-house planning in the offices of first William Burn and then Anthony Salvin (who was Nesfield's uncle). Without Shaw the later history of English domestic architecture would have been very different and he must take much of the credit for the way that English domestic design was so widely admired by the end of the century, as Muthesius's *Das Englische Haus* reveals. Indeed, given that Victorian country-house design begins with Burn and Blore and ends with Shaw and Lutyens it is rather paradoxical that the subject should so often have been presented as one that reached a peak of vitality in the mid-century and then declined: aesthetically speaking, nothing could be less true.

Shaw was also important for the architects whom he trained. Some, such as Ernest Newton, followed in his footsteps, others, notably W. R. Lethaby and Sidney Barnsley, combined Shaw's love of vernacular styles with an idealization of pre-industrial craftsmen learned above all from William Morris. Yet although the Arts and Crafts movement was undoubtedly a powerful influence in English domestic architecture by the turn of the century, it was not alone in the way that it created a potent new image for English country houses rooted in a romantic vision of the countryside. There were plenty of architects and designers who did not share the philosophy of the Arts and Crafts, and in particular its reverence for the independent work of designer-craftsmen, but who were equally skilled at creating houses that implicitly rejected the modern, urban reality of industrialized Britain.

This is evident in the pages of the magazine that more than any other publication distilled this yearning into images, *Country Life*. One of its most influential writers in the years immediately before the First World War, Lawrence Weaver, promoted the Arts and Crafts movement in, for example, the first articles ever published on houses by the movement's greatest architectural hero, Philip Webb. Yet Weaver's interests were balanced by the more belle-lettristic writers, such as C. J. Cornish, who published articles on the immensely photogenic but in no way Arts and Crafts houses and interiors created by such designers as C. E. Kempe. From 1910, the magazine's first architectural editor, Avray Tipping, also revealed an interest in the sensitive historicist work of several late-Victorian architects who stand outside the Arts and Crafts tradition, writing with admiration, for example, about such interiors as the Jacobean-Revival drawing room at Quenby Hall, Leicestershire, designed in 1905 by G. F. Bodley. The work of Bodley, no less than the Arts and Crafts architects, was founded to a large degree on a reaction against the vigour and what was felt as early as the 1860s to be the brashness of early and mid-Victorian architecture. Yet Tipping was capable of regarding even Eaton Hall with dispassionate historical curiosity, writing in 1920 that 'Eaton is a great house, which in its capacity to hold innumerable guests and an infinitude of retainers, imitates an age where the great man's house was self-supportive, self-defensive, self-inclusive.' Victorian houses were dismissed by *Country Life* not solely because they were thought to be ugly. The essential objection to them was that they failed to provide what the magazine sought above all: historic exemplars for modern architects and designers. Simply because of their scale and elaboration, such houses as Eaton could never qualify for that role.

Long before their history came to be written, a sense that the lost world that Victorian country houses represented was in some ways to be regretted is evident in the subtle depiction of Hetton Abbey in Evelyn Waugh's novel *A Handful of Dust* (1934). The owner of this 1860s Gothic house, Tony Last – the surname is, of course, significant – adores Hetton's 'line of battlements against the sky; the central clock tower where quarterly chimes disturbed all but the heaviest sleepers; the ecclesiastical gloom of the great hall, its ceiling groined and painted in diapers of red and gold, supported on shafts of polished granite with vine-wreathed capitals, half-lit by day through lancet windows of armorial stained glass, at night by a vast gasolier of brass and wrought iron.' Waugh's attitude to the house is more detached: everything that Hetton represents throws into relief the shallowness and immorality of the modern, metropolitan world embodied by Tony's wife, Brenda, but it is a lost cause. Tony Last is not destined to enjoy his home but to live

Above: *Scotney Castle, Kent, designed by Anthony Salvin in 1835 and completed in 1843. In 1952 it was inherited by* Country Life*'s architectural editor, Christopher Hussey.*

Left: *A drawing room in Bruton Street, Mayfair, photographed in 1931, when it was specially furnished for an exhibition of mid-Victorian design.*

out his life a prisoner in the Amazon jungle reading Dickens's novels to the crazed Mr Todd.

Yet, as Waugh hints, Hetton Abbey itself was not necessarily doomed, as Tony Last reflects, 'Twenty years ago people had liked half timber and old pewter; now it was urns and colonnades; but the time would come ... when opinion would reinstate Hetton in its proper place. Already it was referred to as "amusing", and a very civil young man had asked permission to photograph it for an architectural review.' That young man must surely have been John Betjeman, assistant editor of the *Architectural Review* from 1930 to 1935. Betjeman's career sums up the rediscovery of Victorian architecture in the second half of the twentieth century, beginning with a rather camp taste for the popular manifestations of Victorian visual culture, from wax fruit under glass domes to fire screens in Berlin wool-work, and ending with a serious

appreciation of its greatest architects. As early as 1931 *Country Life* published a review by John Summerson of an exhibition of Victorian design which took the form of furnishing a house in Bruton Street, Mayfair, as it might have appeared in the 1860s – with startling success, to judge from the photographs. 'The Victorians', wrote Summerson, 'lived in amiable, blissful contentment amid surroundings which, since we are beginning to grow rather fond of them ourselves, we must cease to regard as a species of original sin', but he concluded more seriously, 'A Victorian drawing room is the subject of fashionable curiosity, but Pugin's woodwork in the House of Lords is left to the gaping wonderment of the casual tourist.'

It was over twenty years before the magazine took up that challenge. In the 1950s its architectural editor, Christopher Hussey, who had joined the magazine at the age of twenty-one in 1921, published his three volumes on Georgian houses, based on his articles in *Country Life*. The last, *Late Georgian*, which appeared in 1958, took the subject forward to the early Victorians, with chapters on such houses as Harlaxton. Hussey's interest in this period was in large part prompted by his inheritance in 1952 of one of Anthony Salvin's most attractive small country houses, Scotney Castle in Kent, designed for Hussey's great-grandfather and completed in 1843. The chronological baton was then passed to a new young recruit to the magazine's architectural staff, Mark Girouard, whose series of articles on Victorian houses from the late 1950s onwards were eventually to result in *The Victorian Country House*, conceived of as a successor to Hussey's Georgian volumes.

Girouard was a founding member of the Victorian Society, formed in 1958 to campaign for the preservation of Victorian and Edwardian architecture. Initially its main concerns were urban buildings, and the rapidly increasing rate of demolitions of country houses, many of them Victorian, did not become a priority until after the loss of Eaton Hall in 1961, which raised almost no public protest. By the 1960s, it was realized that intact Victorian country houses were becoming increasingly rare, and Girouard was consulted by the National Trust about the priorities for preservation. It was thanks to the Trust that such major ensembles as Standen and Cragside were saved (both were acquired in 1972). The attention of preservationists was focused to a considerable degree on houses by celebrated architects; the lack of a well-known designer was a disadvantage when Stokesay Court was considered for preservation by English Heritage in 1994: no grant was forthcoming from the National Heritage Memorial Fund for its acquisition, despite the fact that it was a far more intact ensemble than either Standen or Cragside. Hostility to its proposed acquisition by the nation was largely, even at so late a date, prompted by aesthetic distaste, ignoring the very lively interest in Victorian country houses as social documents. The large popular appetite for information about back-stairs life (poorly served by *Country Life* photographs) is evident in the way that the National Trust displays a house such as Lanhydrock in Cornwall, a seventeenth-century house internally completely reconstructed after a fire in 1881; it survives with almost every element of its late-nineteenth-century domestic technology in place.

By the mid-1960s collectors had become interested in the major Victorian designers, from Pugin to Morris. The serious study of William Burges, for example, was first undertaken by Charles Handley-Read; the collection of Victorian decorative arts and sculpture that he formed with his wife, Lavinia, exhibited at the Royal Academy in 1972 after their deaths, inspired a much wider appreciation of avant-garde Victorian design. This enthusiasm also saw a Victorian revival in not only popular culture but also architecture, in such curiosities as Barley Splatt, a house designed for himself by the painter Graham Ovenden, a member of the Brotherhood of Ruralists. This extraordinary example of what may be called an Arts and Crafts version of High Victorian Gothic – furnished with major pieces by Burges and other designers – was published in *Country Life* in 1985.

The rate of attrition of intact Victorian houses remains a cause for concern: the contents of such major houses as Bishops Court and Chanter's House have been dispersed only in the past fifteen years. Yet against this must be set the National Trust's triumph in acquiring Tyntesfield in 2002 with the aid of not just a large grant from the Heritage Lottery Fund but also a very successful public. Even more tellingly, owners of Victorian houses have begun to restore and refurnish them with highly successful results. This book concludes with the renaissance of Arundel Castle in the 1990s. Initiated by the present

Duke and Duchess of Norfolk, it included not only a restoration of the schemes commissioned by the 15th Duke of Norfolk between the 1870s and 1901 but also, under the direction of David Mlinaric, the creation of new interiors, including suites of bedrooms. This triumph reveals that the skills of the great Victorian interior designers are alive and that there are still firms of carvers, painters and upholsterers capable of matching the astonishingly high standards set by their nineteenth-century predecessors.

✣ ✣ ✣

Although it shares a title with Mark Girouard's celebrated work, and similarly is based on *Country Life* articles, this book is quite different in approach, in that it is essentially a commentary on a large selection of the magazine's finest photographs of Victorian country houses. Unlike Dr Girouard's book, it includes Victorian interiors in older houses, but otherwise is narrower in scope, as it deals only with England (with one substantial Welsh exception, Cardiff Castle). This geographical limitation is partly to allow a greater number of less well-known houses to be included and partly also because Victorian houses feature prominently in the books in this series on Scottish and Irish houses, by Ian Gow and Seán O'Reilly respectively. Lutyens has been excluded, as Gavin Stamp has already presented an overview of *Country Life*'s photographs of his work, and I have also striven to avoid too much potential overlap with the planned successor volume in this series, on Arts and Crafts houses. The book focuses tightly on country houses, with only brief excursions to view estate buildings. I have also omitted virtually all consideration of Victorian country-house gardens, which are again the subject of a future volume. Finally, with only one exception, Eaton Hall – an unthinkable omission from a book on the subject – I have chosen only houses that still survive. In part this is because the subject of demolished houses has been so fully dealt with by Giles Worsley in his book *England's Lost Houses*, but also because I wanted to avoid the elegiac tone with which Victorian country houses are so often discussed; what follows is essentially a celebration.

Above: *The billiard room, Arundel Castle, Sussex. In the 1990s, C. A. Buckler's Gothic furniture and fittings, removed in the Second World War, were returned to the room, and a new decorative scheme carried out following a proposal by Buckler. The masonry pattern was designed by the Earl of Arundel, now the 18th Duke of Norfolk.*

Left: *A drawing by the architect Martin Johnson for Barley Splatt, near Bodmin in Cornwall. Designed for himself by the painter Graham Ovenden in collaboration with Johnson, and begun in 1974, the house evokes the architecture of the High Victorian movement.*

1837

REVOLUTION AND REACTION

Queen Victoria's reign opened with a troubled decade. Landowners fought to preserve the tariffs that kept agricultural incomes high, but in 1846 were defeated in the House of Commons. The investment bubble of the railway mania burst and many people lost money. In 1848, a year of revolutions on the Continent, the royal family was evacuated to the Isle of Wight when the Chartist popular reform movement assembled the largest political demonstration ever seen in London. All this was overshadowed by the worst humanitarian disaster to afflict Britain or Ireland since the Black Death in the fourteenth century – the potato famine of 1845–50.

In England, it was an era of Protestant Evangelical millenarianism and popular antipathy to the revival of Roman Catholicism stimulated by Irish immigration. This anxious, febrile atmosphere was embodied in John Martin's vast, apocalyptic paintings, notably *The Deluge*, which was bought in 1837 by Charles Scarisbrick, who was at the time transforming his Lancashire seat, Scarisbrick Hall. His architect was A. W. N. Pugin, whose most celebrated book, *Contrasts* (1836), denounced modern architecture as an embodiment of the moral failings of the age. He called for a return to the ideals of the Middle Ages: for Pugin, the reform of society demanded the revival of Gothic. His beliefs found an echo in the conservative nostalgia of the generation of landowners and politicians known as 'Young England', who, as at Highclere Castle, evoked in romantic form the settled social order of the country's medieval and Tudor past.

Scarisbrick Hall takes many of the tendencies evident in country houses of the 1840s to an extreme. It demonstrates the great wealth of the many landowners who were able to augment agricultural incomes with the proceeds of industrialization. It reveals also the aesthetic confidence of patrons who were not yet inclined instinctively to defer to the rapidly developing professionalization of architects. The scale and confidence of such a mansion as Harlaxton Manor may seem characteristically Victorian, but in its blending of different styles, under the direction of its owner, it is still in some ways Regency in spirit.

Families building or rebuilding their country houses in the 1830s and 1840s had access to a new resource, the vastly increased trade in architectural salvage from Continental houses and churches pillaged in war and revolution. It is possible that by incorporating such elements into the very structure of their houses, the owners of houses such as Wrest Park were asserting the resilience of English landowners, who were maintaining unbroken the traditions that had been so catastrophically severed abroad. Partly against the odds, perhaps, it proved to be a well-founded claim. By the end of the decade the economy was booming and political life was assuming the stability that it would enjoy throughout the long ascendancy of the Liberal Party. The anxious spirit of the 1840s was soon forgotten.

Highclere Castle, Hampshire, seen from Heaven's Gate, an eighteenth-century eye-catcher.

HARLAXTON MANOR, LINCOLNSHIRE

At Harlaxton, the English country house enters the Victorian era to a blazing fanfare of trumpets and drums. This gigantic building rises, utterly unexpectedly, out of gently rolling fields three miles south west of Grantham. From the entrance gates, the approach runs down into a shallow valley, crosses a bridge, skirts the long walls of a kitchen garden, and rises to a baronial gatehouse. The drive then sinks down again before rising to forecourt gates of Baroque pomp, behind which the house soars and spreads, its golden Ancaster stone silhouetted against a dark, wooded ridge.

Harlaxton Manor evokes the prodigy mansions of Elizabethan England, such as Burghley or Wollaton, fused with ideas drawn from Continental architecture of the seventeenth and eighteenth centuries. The use of Tudor or early Stuart models was novel enough for the 1820s, when the house was first conceived, but the creative development of that style as exhibited here was unprecedented. The credit for this must go not to the architects involved, but to their patron, Gregory Gregory. Harlaxton was the all-consuming interest of his life. He never married and despised his heir, a distant cousin; country pursuits bored him and he disliked entertaining. The house was for him an end in itself. As J. C. Loudon wrote in 1840, Gregory 'may be said to have embodied himself in the edifice, and to live in every feature of it, as a planter may be said to live in every tree he has planted and a florist in every flower he has raised.'

Born in 1786, Gregory Gregory-Williams (he changed his name when he inherited the Harlaxton estate from his grandmother in 1822) came from a prosperous gentry family with land in Nottinghamshire and Lincolnshire. His father had begun the industrial development of the family's Denton estate, on the outskirts of Nottingham, providing a new source of revenue that helped to pay for Harlaxton Manor. Although historians are sometimes surprised that a house on this scale – it cost around £100,000 – was built by a relatively modest landowner with an income of £12,000 a year, it was not completed until nearly thirty years after Gregory had first planned it. With no dependants, he could easily have paid for it out of his income. This leisurely time scale may also reflect the delight that he took in his undertaking; it certainly allowed him to make major changes as the project progressed.

The principal, and much decayed, house on the Harlaxton estate had been remodelled in the early seventeenth century. Initially, Gregory simply wanted a more spacious and convenient house that would reflect the style of the old, and reuse some of its architectural elements and fittings. However, he waited for almost ten years after inheriting the estate before he began work, partly to accumulate a

The house rising up behind its forecourt. The massive gateway and lodges, among the most Baroque elements of Harlaxton Manor, were probably designed by David Bryce, who worked in William Burn's office.

building fund and partly to complete the collection around which the house would be designed.

The death of his father in 1814, followed a year afterwards by the end of the Napoleonic Wars, gave Gregory both the means and the opportunity to collect on a grand scale. He is believed to have had a post at the British Embassy in Paris, positioning him perfectly to acquire not works of art – he had surprisingly little interest in painting or sculpture for its own sake – but fittings and furnishings, which could be incorporated into the house that he was probably planning even before his grandmother died. Thanks to the flood of works brought onto the market by revolution and war, prices were low and Gregory was able to buy panelling, chimneypieces, furniture and tapestries in great quantity.

In 1831 he was ready to start on the house and asked the architect Anthony Salvin for designs. Although he had been in practice for barely seven years, Salvin had already demonstrated a scholarly understanding of the Elizabethan and Jacobean sources that interested Gregory, who had undertaken his own study tour of houses of the period. Salvin's drawings show that he quickly established the basic plan and massing of the house. As the project developed, he introduced much richer ornament of Continental derivation, some of it taken from seventeenth-century pattern books by Wendel Dietterlin and Hans Vredeman de Vries that Gregory owned.

In 1835, just as Gregory's attention was turning to the interiors, Salvin went on an architectural tour of Germany. This may have been

Above: *The Gold Drawing Room, one of the principal interiors created under William Burn's direction. It incorporates authentic French eighteenth-century panelling – an idea that looks forward to such houses as Waddesdon Manor in Buckinghamshire.*

Left: *The great hall as it appeared in 1957, adapted to serve as the chapel of the novitiate of the English Jesuits, who then owned Harlaxton. Its overall form is based on Jacobean precedents, but the crouching figures, carrying the brackets that support the roof, suggest Continental inspiration.*

prompted by the way that his patron's ideas were developing, towards a fusion of English models with foreign ones. Although the great hall, for example, is recognisably derived from that at Audley End in Essex, its roof trusses are supported by muscular atlantes of a type common in German Baroque architecture. But even this does not prepare one for the breathtaking surprise of the Cedar Staircase. Rising through three storeys to a painted sky, this astonishingly theatrical *tour de force* begins with more atlantes on the ground floor, above which trumpet-playing *putti* bearing scallop shells fly amid billowing plaster curtains. At the top are figures of Father Time (with real scythes), carrying flags depicting a plan of the house, and a portrait of Gregory.

In 1838 Gregory abruptly dismissed Salvin, for reasons that have never been explained. It is possible that he had come to feel that Salvin was not capable of creating interiors that reflected Gregory's imagined ones. Salvin's replacement was the Scottish country-house specialist William Burn, who possessed the skill and experience to weave reused architectural fittings into French Baroque and Rococo interiors, as Harlaxton's principal reception rooms reveal. However, he never designed anything else as magnificent as the Cedar Staircase, which embodied Gregory's own ideas, perhaps inspired by Bavarian Baroque architecture.

The house was complete by 1851, when Gregory is first documented as living there, but he did not enjoy it for long, dying in 1854. He had unsuccessfully tried to break the entail on the estate, hoping to leave it to his close friend and neighbour Sir William Welby of Denton, but was only able to leave part of the contents to him (the rest was sold in 1878). Harlaxton Manor remained in Gregory's family until 1936, when it narrowly escaped demolition. Having been for several years the novitiate of the English Jesuits (in whose possession it was when *Country Life* photographed the house for Christopher Hussey's 1957 articles for the magazine), it is now owned by the University of Evansville, Indiana.

Two views of the Cedar Staircase, Harlaxton's most spectacular – and unexpected – interior. Its makers are unknown, although the principal firm of English architectural plasterworkers, Francis Bernasconi & Sons, undoubtedly possessed the skills to achieve such a tour de force.

HIGHCLERE CASTLE, HAMPSHIRE

In 1834 the medieval Houses of Parliament were destroyed by fire, a disaster that was to shape one of the most successful architectural careers in early Victorian Britain. On 29 February 1836, it was announced that the competition for designing a new Palace of Westminster had been won by Charles Barry. He was not unknown, as four years earlier his first major public building, the Travellers' Club in Pall Mall, had been completed to great acclaim. The club was designed in an innovatory Florentine Renaissance style, establishing Barry as a creative interpreter of the Classical tradition. His design for the new Houses of Parliament revealed that he was equally accomplished as a designer of Gothic buildings.

Barry claimed little archaeological understanding of medieval architecture, and so he called on the precocious Gothic designer A. W. N. Pugin to provide the detailing for the drawings for the Westminster competition. Pugin would eventually supply designs for not only the building's architectural ornament but also most of its fittings and furniture. Partly because Pugin's single-minded belief in Gothic as the one true style is so compelling, Barry's ability to switch from one style to another has sometimes led him to be regarded as shallow by comparison, or at best essentially a Classicist, who when called upon to design a Gothic or Tudor building simply draped appropriate ornament over a Classical structure.

It is true that the large country-house practice that Barry came to enjoy – in part as a result of his Westminster fame – reveals a mission to create a new, flexible Italianate idiom, seen to great effect, for example, at Shrubland Park, Suffolk (see pages 56–59). Yet when he turned to Elizabethan forms at Highclere Castle, the result was very successful, and reveals that Barry had a sophisticated sense of how historic styles could be adapted to modern needs.

Highclere was commissioned by the youthful Henry Herbert, 3rd Earl of Carnarvon, whose romantic enthusiasms (he wrote poetry and plays) made him dissatisfied with the Classical eighteenth-century house that he had inherited in 1833, set in a beautiful park just outside Newbury. The Carnarvons were a political dynasty, leading members of the Tory Party in the House of Lords, and it has been suggested that the choice of an Elizabethan style for Highclere was intended to evoke the aristocratic traditions that the Tories felt were being undermined by Whig legislation – the family opposed both the Reform Bill of 1832, which extended the parliamentary franchise, and the 1846 repeal of the Corn Laws, which ended protectionism for British agriculture. However, the history of the design suggests that the style was chosen just as much for practical reasons.

In origin a cadet branch of the Herbert family of Wilton House, Wiltshire, the Earls of Carnarvon were not especially wealthy, and the 3rd Earl's original intention was simply to aggrandize the house in a

The south and east fronts of Highclere Castle. The very regular arrangement of the windows is the only clue that Charles Barry simply encased an eighteenth-century house.

Above: *The rib-vaulted entrance hall, one of only two interiors in the house by Charles Barry. The tiled floor was designed by William Butterfield, who carried out minor alterations to the house in 1863.*

Right: *The saloon. The arrangement of a double-height room opening into corridors at first-floor level was Barry's, but all the decorative detail was designed by Thomas Allom.*

Classical style. Barry's first drawings show that he intended rusticating its ground floor and adding belvederes to the corners. Lord Carnarvon seems to have felt that was not quite enough, for Barry then suggested adding a tall, central tower, intended to crown a new triple-height Italianate saloon. Perhaps because this design recalled an Elizabethan prodigy house, such as Wollaton in Nottinghamshire, Barry proposed recasting the exterior of house in late-sixteenth-century form, richly embellished with turrets, pinnacles, strapwork ornament and heraldic sculpture.

He did not primarily employ this idiom – which he called 'Anglo-Italian' – for visual or associational reasons. His client's limited purse was an important factor. As Barry's son, Alfred, explained in his 1867 memoir of his father, the choice of such a flexible style meant that 'not only were the main walls preserved, with scarcely any extension of the building or plan, but even the secondary features were kept intact. In no case was the level of any floor or the opening of a window changed.'

Somewhat to his architect's annoyance, Lord Carnarvon enjoyed asking his friends for their opinion on the designs, and was delighted when Prince Albert praised the model made for Barry as 'a very fine specimen'. The model-maker, Thomas Dighton, reported back that Prince Albert 'objected to the windows, that the openings were too great, and on my asking if he thought a Mullion and Transom being introduced would remedy the objections he answered "decidedly".'

Despite the ingenious retention of so much of the old house, Lord Carnarvon worried that the expense of the rebuilding was too great, writing to Barry that: 'I am very anxious to effect your beautiful design but am very fearful of erecting the shell and being unable to complete the house so as to live in it.' It may have been partly for reasons of economy that Barry gave up the idea of a saloon rising through the full height of the house, crowned by a tower, in favour of a double-height room, with an off-centre tower over the staircase. Nonetheless, Lord Carnarvon's fears were justified: when he died in 1849 the interiors had barely been begun and he left a very substantial overdraft.

As a result, the only interiors by Barry are the Gothic rib-vaulted entrance hall and the staircase hall. The remainder of the rooms were designed by Thomas Allom, best known as an architectural perspectivist (his watercolours of Barry's designs for Highclere were exhibited at the Royal Academy in 1840), and were not completed until the 1860s. The most memorable of his interiors is the top-lit saloon, fitted out with Gothic plasterwork, Spanish leather hangings and eighteenth-century tapestries to wonderfully rich effect. The splendid and well-preserved library, reminiscent of that at Barry's Travellers' Club, still strongly evokes the intimate social atmosphere of mid-Victorian political life, for which country houses were an important setting. Since the late nineteenth century few changes have been made to the house, which remains the seat of the Earls of Carnarvon.

The library. Its design and fittings, notably the mahogany-grained and gilded columns, are reminiscent of Barry's London clubs.

SCARISBRICK HALL, LANCASHIRE

For most of the nineteenth century anyone who wanted to buy old furniture or architectural fittings would eventually find their way to Wardour Street in Soho, London. By 1850 it had twenty-three shops dealing in such material. Part of the attraction of the area to these dealers was its long-established cabinet-making and metalworking trades, and hence the easy availability of craftsmen to repair old pieces. Such intervention often encompassed outright fakery: by the 1880s the term 'Wardour Street English' was used to describe affectedly archaic diction – 'a perfectly modern article with a sham appearance of the real antique about it.' Yet when the trade settled in Wardour Street, such deception was scarcely needed. Thanks to the destruction or despoliation of so many churches and monastic buildings on the Continent, there was a seemingly endless supply of genuine material with a new appeal to patrons and architects inspired by the Romantic Movement and the Gothic Revival to give their buildings an instant air of antiquity.

One of Wardour Street's busiest dealers was Edward Hull. Perhaps his greatest client was a Lancashire landowner, Charles Scarisbrick, who in 1833 inherited Scarisbrick Hall at Ormskirk, near Southport. At once he started to buy old carvings in great quantity from Hull and other dealers to embellish the house, spending an astonishing £5,500 between 1836 and 1846. Around 1837 he asked Hull to recommend an architect who could supply designs for a Gothic garden seat and a fireplace. Hull put him in touch with A. W. N. Pugin, who was only twenty-five and had completed only one building – his own home. Yet Pugin had designed furniture for George IV at Windsor Castle when he was only fifteen, and in 1836, a year after his conversion to Roman Catholicism, he had published an extraordinary architectural manifesto, *Contrasts*, which declared that Gothic was the only Christian style and its revival the only hope for nineteenth-century architecture. In 1837 nobody in Europe had a more creative understanding of Gothic design than Pugin, who hungered for chances to give his knowledge physical embodiment.

Above: *The entrance front from the south, photographed in 1957. To the left of the tower is the house, remodelled by first Slater and Rickman in the 1820s and then by A. W. N. Pugin between 1837 and 1845; the tower and the stable court to its right were added in the 1860s by his son, E. W. Pugin.*

Right: *The north porch, added by A. W. N. Pugin in about 1838.*

Charles Scarisbrick demonstrated his strong and somewhat hard personality when, after his elder brother died in 1833, he instituted a legal case to exclude his sisters from any claim on the estate, finally defeating them in the House of Lords. The Scarisbricks, who had been seated here since the twelfth century, had maintained their Catholic faith after the Reformation. The inevitable reclusiveness that such a choice necessitated was reflected in the physical isolation of Scarisbrick Hall, surrounded by the flat expanses of Martin Mere, drained in the eighteenth century. It was echoed also in Scarisbrick's withdrawal from society, prompted by his unorthodox family life: he never married but lived in London with his mistress, Mary Anne Braithwaite, and their three children. In the circumstances, it is perhaps surprising that he devoted so much energy to Scarisbrick Hall, but he seems to have had few other outlets for the substantial income he enjoyed from the development of Southport and his Lancashire coalmines. As Pugin's biographer, Rosemary Hill, writes of Scarisbrick, 'like so many early Victorian magnates, he was as romantic on the one side as he was materialistic on the other, spinning the profits of coal and boarding houses into extravagant Gothic fantasy.'

Two views of the great hall, photographed in 2002. A. W. N. Pugin designed the timber-framed roof and embellished the room with trophies from Charles Scarisbrick's spectacular collection of antiquarian carvings. Scarisbrick's initials are emblazoned in the tiled floor.

His remodelling of Scarisbrick Hall continued the work of his brother. In 1812–16 Thomas Scarisbrick had employed John Slater, a Liverpool joiner who practised as an architect, to restore and enlarge the timber-framed Elizabethan structure. Working with the architect Thomas Rickman, a pioneer scholar of Gothic, Slater encased the house in stone and altered and extended the west wing, which contains the principal rooms. They also removed the ceiling of the drawing room to recreate the house's double-storey great hall.

Charles Scarisbrick gave Pugin only limited freedom to alter the exterior, which he did largely by giving it a more picturesque silhouette, with such features as a louvre over the hall. His major additions were the north and south porches. Inside, however, Pugin seems to have had a free hand to create some of the early Gothic Revival's most elaborate surviving interiors, using Scarisbrick's vast

store of antiquarian carvings. Here, Pugin put to good use his experience designing stage sets for historical dramas in London theatres. To the great hall he added a timber-framed roof, a gallery, a throne and a mighty chimneypiece. On an end wall he installed one of Scarisbrick's largest trophies, a huge Flemish carved wooden altarpiece depicting the mocking of Christ. To later Victorian eyes – and also to Pugin – it was incongruous to employ ecclesiastical fittings for such purposes, but Scarisbrick seems to have felt no compunction about it, to judge from his use of wings from altarpieces to form the double doors between the library and dining room.

Although magnificent, the interiors created by Pugin out of these rich materials were only the beginning for him: he hoped to persuade his client to extend the house on a baronial scale, complete with a chapel and a bell tower – his design for the tower prefigures the one at the Palace of Westminster, on which Pugin was then collaborating. But Scarisbrick showed no interest in such extravagance.

A. W. N. Pugin died in 1852, followed eight years later by Scarisbrick, who left instructions that his surviving sister, the seventy-two-year-old Anne, Lady Hunloke, was not to be told of his death. But she could not be denied for ever, and, having changed her name to Lady Scarisbrick, took possession of Scarisbrick Hall in great state in 1861. Clearly determined to stamp her mark on the house, she turned to Pugin's eldest son, the twenty-six-year-old Edward Welby Pugin, who had inherited his father's practice. They embarked on extending the house, very much on the lines that A. W. N. Pugin had contemplated. Indeed, Lady Scarisbrick even added the tower that he had proposed, redesigned to be yet loftier, but without a clock – and so with no practical function at all.

After Lady Scarisbrick died in 1872, the house passed to her daughter and left Scarisbrick ownership. In 1962 it was bought for demolition, but was saved; it is now a private school.

Above: *The Red Drawing Room, formerly the library. Pugin's designs for the chimneypiece and ceiling date from 1837.*

Right: *The King's Room. It is almost impossible to tell where the antiquarian carvings end and Pugin's framework for them begins.*

WREST PARK, BEDFORDSHIRE

Although English patrons have for centuries looked to France for guidance in architecture and the decorative arts, the flowering of French influence in England in the 1820s and 1830s had a particular flavour of nostalgia. The French monarchy and aristocracy had largely been obliterated, their palaces and châteaux pillaged and their collections thrown onto the market. By contrast, the landowning classes in England were flourishing. There was a sense, therefore, that the English aristocracy was self-consciously continuing the severed traditions of its French counterparts – an idea given physical expression in the new Francophile interiors they created out of the paintings, sculpture, bronzes, furniture, tapestries and porcelain displaced by revolution and war. Ambitious purchasers even acquired fine *boiseries* with which to fit out their new rooms in a French style.

Often, as for example at Belvoir Castle, Rutland, such interiors were created within architectural frameworks that were emphatically English – 'Saxon' (or Romanesque as we would say) at Belvoir; Gothic elsewhere. At Wrest Park, however, the influence of France extended to the architecture: indeed, England has few tributes to French eighteenth-century traditions so wholehearted and enjoyable. Could anything be more unexpected in rural Bedfordshire than this evocation of the vanished splendours of the *ancien régime*?

The house's architect was its owner, Thomas, Earl de Grey, who inherited the estate in 1833. He stands in a long tradition of English landowners who have designed their own homes, although few accomplished anything on the scale of Wrest Park. It is the last triumph of the amateur aristocratic architect at the dawn of the age

Above: *Wrest Park's garden front in 1904. It is derived in part from a design published in 1737 by Jacques-François Blondel.*

Right: *The view from the garden front, looking out over the Victorian parterre. In the distance, at the end of the eighteenth-century long water, is Thomas Archer's Baroque pavilion, completed in 1711.*

of professionalism, as Earl de Grey may have realized: in 1834, the second year of building at Wrest, he became the first president of the newly formed Institute of British Architects. The style of his new house is in part a response to the great glory of the park, the formal garden laid out for the 1st Duke of Kent between 1702 and 1740, which is strongly French in flavour. Earl de Grey enhanced it by laying out a parterre on axis with the eighteenth-century long water, which culminates in a masterpiece of English Baroque architecture: the pavilion designed by Thomas Archer in 1709–11.

Earl de Grey's extensive travels in France in the 1820s fostered a deep love of the country's early-eighteenth-century architecture. He made a close study of not only buildings of the era but also architects' drawings and books, of which he formed a substantial library. Wrest Park ingeniously synthesizes a wide range of sources, from Parisian *hôtels* to large châteaux, into a convincing whole. Its architect paid a graceful tribute to his sources in the overdoor beneath the house's main staircase: figures representing painting and architecture are seated on books labelled 'Blondel', 'Mansard' and 'Le Pautre'.

In some rooms, Earl de Grey incorporated authentic French *boiseries*, but most of the decoration and furnishing of the house were executed by English craftsmen, under the direction of a clerk-of-works, James Clephane. The Earl was determined to give the female overdoor figures a voluptuousness that seemed not to come naturally to English artists: he told his daughter that the sculptors' 'ideas of female beauty in point of roundness of form did not correspond with mine, and I was forced to add to all their prominent parts.'

On Earl de Grey's death in 1859 the estate was inherited by his daughter Anne, and became a secondary seat for the family of her husband, Earl Cowper. In 1946 the park was acquired by the Ministry of Public Building and Works. The house was acquired by English Heritage in 2006.

Above: *The drawing room in 1904. Its Rococo pier-glasses and furniture were probably supplied to Earl de Grey by a London firm, Dowbiggin & Co., in 1839.*

Left: *The staircase hall, which rises the full height of the building, was used by Earl de Grey as a reception room. Full-length eighteenth-century family portraits are set into the walls.*

1850

BATTLE OF THE STYLES

When Queen Victoria opened the Great Exhibition on 1 May 1851 anxieties about the future, which had dominated the previous decade, were forgotten in the outburst of enthusiasm for such a bold statement of progressive optimism. It is not surprising that there are echoes of this extraordinary event in country houses – after all, Joseph Paxton's inspired conception of the Crystal Palace was derived in large part from his experiments in iron and glass construction for the glass houses at Chatsworth. As well as making significant purchases of works shown at the Great Exhibition, the owner of Flintham Hall in Nottinghamshire built a great barrel-vaulted conservatory, which presides over the house like a miniature Crystal Palace.

As the world's first-ever international display of art and manufactures, the Great Exhibition also brought home to British architects and designers the extraordinary variety of styles that were available for modern consumption. As Regency architecture demonstrates, stylistic eclecticism was hardly a novelty, but it was not an issue that had caused any great anxiety or even profound reflection in England before the 1840s.

Laissez-faire attitudes to stylistic choice were first seriously challenged by A. W. N. Pugin, whose belief that Gothic was a style with a Christian and moral imperative deeply influenced the young architects of the 1840s and 1850s, most notably William Butterfield. Picking up hints from Pugin's later writings and buildings, they sought to develop Gothic into a style fit for all modern purposes. Among the most ardent believer in the necessity of Gothic was George Gilbert Scott. Since his eventual success in the 1856 competition for the new Foreign Office came at the expense of sacrificing his original Gothic proposals for an Italianate Classical design, it is widely believed that the decade witnessed a 'Battle of the Styles' between Gothic and Classical.

Yet as the five houses described in the following chapter reveal, the range of stylistic possibility in the 1850s was far wider than that. Many – and probably most – estate owners embarking on new houses, such as Lord Harrowby at Sandon, wanted buildings that were Elizabethan or Jacobean in stylistic derivation, partly because it was a distinctively English idiom that allowed for flexibility of plan and picturesque variety of form without the Catholic, High Church or feudal implications of Gothic. Yet even where a patron seemed to have good reason to embrace Gothic, as in the 4th Duke of Northumberland's rebuilding of Alnwick Castle, his choice of the style came with reservations, as the interiors were fitted out in a Cinquecento manner. Indeed, when Victoria's reign is surveyed as a whole, it is arguable that the most distinctive feature of country-house architecture is not the use of Gothic, but the resilience of inventive, Italianate forms of Classicism.

1860

The inner courtyard of Alnwick Castle, Northumberland, remodelled by Anthony Salvin in 1854–56.

ALNWICK CASTLE, NORTHUMBERLAND

Stupendous although it is, Harlaxton Manor was not the greatest country-house commission that Anthony Salvin received. In 1854 he began the remodelling of Alnwick Castle, the mighty ancestral fortress of the Percy family, Dukes of Northumberland. By the time that Salvin had finished, in 1866, the 4th Duke had spent £295,000. He could easily afford it: he enjoyed an income of £120,000 a year from agriculture and coalmining. Architecturally, Salvin was given a free hand, but on one major element, the design of the interiors, he was completely overruled by the Duke. Salvin regretted this, but we hardly can, given the magnificence of the results.

When the Duke succeeded his brother in 1847 he inherited a castle rescued from ruin by his grandfather, who in the 1760s and 1770s had employed Henry Keene, James Paine and lastly Robert Adam to restore it. The result was a pioneering exercise in using the Gothic style to reassert a feudal presence, but from a Victorian point of view the building had many problems. The principal rooms, in the castle's keep, were laid out as an enfilade, with no access corridor and no separate circulation for servants. Meals arrived at the dining room after being conveyed from the kitchen across the gateway and up a circular stair. But the Duke's motives for rebuilding were not solely practical: he hankered after a castle with a more romantic silhouette than the eighteenth century (or the Middle Ages) had felt inclined to provide. In an assessment of Salvin's work at Alnwick published in 1857, T. L. Donaldson, Professor of Architecture at University College, London, commented that the Duke regretted the way that the previous restoration 'had caused it to lose many striking features ... depriving it of much of that original dignity and variety of effect, which it had doubtless possessed in ancient times.'

Among the scholars whom the Duke consulted before beginning work to remedy these deficiencies was the antiquary Charles

Above: *The guard chamber, at the head of the stairs leading to the state rooms.*

Left: *The keep, seen through the gatehouse archway. This view shows two of Salvin's principal additions: the tall, oblong Prudhoe Tower and the apsed chapel to its right.*

Hartshorne, who admired Salvin's careful repair of Caernarfon Castle, carried out in 1844–48. It may have been at his recommendation that in February 1849 the Duke asked Salvin to undertake a survey of Alnwick Castle. In the same month the Duke visited not only Caernarfon but also Peckforton Castle in Cheshire, an entirely new castle in thirteenth-century style, designed by Salvin in 1844 for Lord Tollemache. In 1854, after a long tour of Italy that was to have a major influence on the project, the Duke approved Salvin's designs for remodelling Alnwick.

Because the castle had been so altered in the eighteenth century, and now had to be adapted to modern needs, Salvin felt no obligation to adopt an archaeological approach. Two towers on the north-west angle of the keep were demolished and replaced by the much higher rectangular Prudhoe Tower. The tower to its south was rebuilt as a chapel with a polygonal apse. Salvin linked the reception rooms (which largely retained their eighteenth-century plan, although Adam's work was swept away) by a corridor corbelled out into the inner courtyard. The Duke needed a large room in which to entertain his tenantry and his first idea was to extend the keep with a new great hall in the outer bailey, where he believed one might have existed in medieval times. In the end, Salvin was asked to create a guest hall in the stable yard, making a greater separation between the Duke's private realm and his public responsibilities.

A twelfth-century gateway leads into the keep's inner courtyard, largely rebuilt by Salvin. The impressive quality of the masonry achieved by the builders, Smith and Appleford, is enhanced by Salvin's eschewal of decoration: the forms are kept plain and crisp. This may have been in part to create a strong contrast with the interiors, to which Salvin designed a carefully controlled approach. As at Harlaxton, a low, dark entrance hall opens into a spacious staircase. This ascends to a guard room and then to an anteroom, which leads on one side into a large library, occupying the whole of the first floor of the Prudhoe Tower, and on the other into the state rooms – but the design of those rooms was not his.

The Duke gave a great deal of thought to the way that the castle was to be fitted out. At Peckforton, Salvin had created stony Gothic interiors to match the stony Gothic exterior. The result was impressive, but chilly. In Italy the Duke was struck by the way that medieval fortresses had been adapted to contain Renaissance and Baroque interiors. He decided to adopt this idea at Alnwick, on the grounds that it was 'not so peculiar as to be a variance with contemporary usage or feeling.' While the Duke was in Rome, Cardinal Antonelli introduced him to the Classical architect and archaeologist Luigi Canina. Salvin was asked to send measured drawings of Alnwick's reception rooms so that Canina and his assistant, Giovanni Montiroli, could design a decorative scheme based on High Renaissance Italian precedents.

The Red Drawing room, photographed in 1988. The Carrara marble chimneypiece was carved by Giuseppe Nucci, and the painted decoration is by Alessandro Mantovani, who was responsible for similar work in the Papal palaces in Rome.

This must have been difficult for Salvin, but he was retained by the Duke to oversee the group of Italian craftsmen whom Canina had assembled to execute the work, following Montiroli's full-scale drawings. These included principally the sculptor Giovanni Taccalozzi, responsible for most of the marble chimneypieces, the woodcarver Leone Bulletti and Alessandro Mantovani, who painted the Renaissance ornament in the friezes. Canina died suddenly in 1855, leaving Montiroli in charge of the scheme's artistic direction. The Duke hoped that the presence of these sculptors, carvers and painters in England would help to improve the quality of British craftsmanship and 'promote a more extensive system of artistic instruction in England in that style of decoration.' He paid for drawing lessons for the British workmen brought in to assist the Italians and arranged for the carvers to visit the International Exhibition in London in 1862.

The result was some of the most impressive interiors of their date in Europe, in which coffered ceilings, sculptured marble chimney-pieces, painted decoration, furniture and upholstery are combined in sumptuous ensembles that do indeed evoke a great Roman palazzo. They form a splendidly appropriate backdrop to the Camuccini collection of Italian Old Masters, which included masterpieces by Titian and Raphael, acquired by the 4th Duke *en bloc* in 1856. Nonetheless, these rooms had a poor critical reception. At a meeting of the Royal Institute of British Architects in 1857, George Gilbert Scott declared that 'his Grace has made one of the greatest and most lamentable mistakes which has been made in the present day' in not creating medieval interiors in harmony with the castle's architecture. Salvin confessed that he had had his 'doubts as to the propriety and practicality of introducing Italian art into a Border castle ... My own wish would have been to devise Mediaeval decorations to a plan consistent with modern requirements. I must here observe that I do not for a moment admit what many opponents of the style urge against it, that because the doors, the windows and the ceilings are Mediaeval, therefore, the floors must be covered with rushes, and the furniture benches.'

These criticisms reflect the growing determination of Gothic Revival architects to establish the style as one fit for all modern purposes. They also embody the way that the restoration of medieval buildings was becoming more scholarly and purist. In addition, Scott's words hint at a feeling that architects, newly confident in their professionalism, knew best – or at least better than their clients. It seems unlikely that such complaints ruffled the Duke, who had accomplished exactly what he had set out to do – in the words of Professor Donaldson, 'To surround himself with noble and imposing associations', which 'was in his Grace's mind a duty he owed [to] himself ... and to those who should succeed to a title consecrated in the annals of the country.' His successors in the dukedom, who in 2009 celebrated the 600th anniversary of the Percy family's purchase of Alnwick Castle, have preserved intact what he achieved.

The dining room, hung with family portraits. The chimneypiece is by Taccalozzi and Nucci.

SHRUBLAND PARK, SUFFOLK

It is a peculiarity of Charles Barry's career that although he had a large and very influential country-house practice he was never responsible for an entirely new large house. All his commissions were remodellings of existing buildings, with the exception of the Duke and Duchess of Sutherland's Cliveden in Buckinghamshire, which he designed in 1849, but even there Barry was forced to keep to the foundations of the previous house on the site, which had been destroyed by fire. Both the houses that his son, Alfred, recalled as his father's favourites, Highclere Castle and Shrubland Park, were recastings of eighteenth-century houses.

Barry's patron at Shrubland was Sir William Fowle Middleton, who had inherited the estate in 1829. His wife was a sister of Edward Cust, a judge in the competition for the new Houses of Parliament and a great supporter of the architect during its building. Middleton agreed with Barry that the house, designed by James Paine and built in 1770–72, was a 'quakerish even maudlin building' that largely failed to take advantage of its spectacular site (especially spectacular in Suffolk): a high ridge overlooking the broad Gipping valley, north west of Ipswich. Barry set about its transformation in 1849.

The house had already been altered for Middleton once, as recently as 1831–33, by John Gandy Deering, a pupil of James Wyatt and a noted authority on Classical architecture. Even Barry was prepared to admit that his changes were successful. Gandy Deering had created a new entrance on the east front, to replace Paine's on the west, allowing a terrace to be built along the west front, from which the magnificent view could be enjoyed. Barry's interior changes included the addition of galleries for Middleton's collections and the decoration of some rooms in French Rococo style. Outside, he completed Gandy Deering's remodelling by replacing Paine's pediments with balustrades and raising a belvedere over the low tower that his

Above: *The garden front. Charles Barry drastically remodelled the house designed by James Paine in 1770. The belvedere tower over the south wing, designed for enjoyment of the spectacular view, was an influential feature of many of Barry's Classical houses.*

Left: *The steps that lead down from the house to the Fountain Garden on the lowest terrace, a design inspired by Italian Renaissance gardens seen by Barry on his Grand Tour. These photographs were taken in 1953.*

predecessor had added to the south wing. This was one of three towers that he originally proposed, but the Middletons preferred the picturesque asymmetry of one. The result suggests an Italian villa like those that Barry had sketched in Tuscany and Rome during his time in Italy in 1819–20. The resemblance was made complete by the architectural garden that he laid out in front of the house.

The existing terrace was enclosed by a new balustrade and the hill below it was carved into further terraces, the lowest extending a mile from north to south. This incorporates a Swiss cottage, a French garden and a fountain garden, originally the framework for elaborate carpet bedding. The terrace is reached from the house by a monumental staircase descending in four flights with a panache that recalls the Villa d'Este at Tivoli. At its head is a richly ornamented archway of eighteenth-century inspiration. This looks down to a triple-arched loggia in an Italian sixteenth-century style on the lowest terrace; below that, steps lead down into the parkland. This carefully planned transition from the architectural platform surrounding the house to untouched nature far below was immediately recognized as masterly and was much imitated, as was the innovation of the planting of the slope on either side of the staircase as a wilderness.

When he died childless in 1860, Sir William Middleton – most unusually – created a trust to provide an income of £2,000 a year to be devoted to the upkeep of the 65-acre garden. In 1882 the estate passed by marriage to the 4th Lord de Saumarez. From the 1960s onwards the house was occupied by a health clinic, but the gardens were maintained and until 2006, when the estate was placed on the market, were open to the public.

Above: *The archway at the head of the steps. In the distance is the Italianate loggia on the lowest terrace, which marks the point where the garden melts into the park.*

Right: *The view down the steps to the Fountain Garden, with some of the carpet beds visible. In the 1880s the original planting of Barry's garden was simplified with advice from the celebrated gardener William Robinson.*

SANDON HALL, STAFFORDSHIRE

In June 1848 Sandon Hall, the Staffordshire seat of the 2nd Earl of Harrowby, was gutted by a fire started by careless plumbers mending lead-work on the roof of the eighteenth-century house. The servants rushed to rescue the contents, with a tragic result: a house carpenter, Frank Perkin, was crushed to death when a cornice collapsed in the billiard room. But almost all the paintings and furnishings – including even the plate glass windows and chimneypieces – were saved, thanks to the exertions of the estate staff, who laboured for thirty hours, sustained only by beer ('so exhausted *and* intoxicated' wrote the Countess of Harrowby after surveying the ruin). When news of the fire reached him, Lord Harrowby was in London, dining at Lambeth Palace: 'I need hardly tell you how quietly Papa took it', wrote his wife in a family letter. His calmness may have been partly explained by the knowledge that the house was well insured.

Lord Sandon, the Harrowbys' eldest son, asked Earl de Grey, President of the Royal Institute of British Architects (and designer of Wrest Park) to recommend an architect for a replacement house. He suggested the builder Thomas Cubitt, who proposed rebuilding the house in a Classical style, but after consideration the Harrowbys decided to consult William Burn. It cannot have been a difficult choice. Burn was the most successful country-house architect of the time, who in the course of a career lasting nearly sixty years designed over a hundred new country houses and remodelled many more. Although trained in London by the eminent Neo-Classical architect Robert Smirke, he set up practice in his native Edinburgh in 1811 or 1812. He specialized in a reserved form of Jacobean, often with Scottish inflections, but his clients were attracted less by his stylistic

Above: *Sandon Hall's north front, set behind an entrance forecourt, photographed in 1988.*

Right: *The hall, seen from the staircase. Its furthest division originally housed a billiard table.*

facility and more by his well-deserved reputation for excellent planning and ability to stay within budget.

Burn's career was transformed by the commission to complete Harlaxton Manor, which first brought him to the attention of English clients. Within a few years he was working at Eaton Hall for the Marquess of Westminster, at Arundel Castle for the Duke of Norfolk and at Holkham Hall for the Earl of Leicester. The Harrowbys may well have been aware of another Staffordshire commission, the Jacobean-style Calwich Abbey, designed in 1846, but in any case, Lord Harrowby, an eminent politician who had four times been elected MP for Liverpool, would have known a great number of Burn's patrons. So successful was Burn in obtaining English commissions that in 1844 he moved to London, leaving his Edinburgh office in the hands of his partner David Bryce. By 1849 their relationship was becoming tense, as Bryce not unreasonably resented Burn's continuing to take commissions from Scottish clients. The strain this was putting on Burn's practice may help to explain why Sandon Hall proved such a fraught project for him. The house is exceptional in his work for surviving intact with its original furnishings in the hands of his client's descendants. Less happily, it is also unusual for the degree to which Burn fell out with his patron.

The project got off to a slightly uncomfortable start when – it having been ascertained that there was no appreciable difference in cost between a Classical and a Tudor design – Lord Sandon, who was only eighteen, produced his own Jacobean design for the house. Burn was accustomed to deflecting unwelcome suggestions by his clients, and wrote to Lord Harrowby in January 1849 that if executed the designs 'would have led to an expenditure much beyond what is contemplated, and I also think to a house considerably too long for the grounds.' Burn had a customary formula for presenting designs, a set of small-scale ink and wash plans and a perspective drawing, and was so experienced that he was used to them being accepted with only minor changes. The Harrowbys were not so accommodating. In the first place, there was prolonged discussion about how much of the old house should be retained. This was partly a matter of a cost – and, as it turned out, cost was to matter a lot. But the real issue was their inability to settle on a plan.

Above: *The drawing room. The fireplace was salvaged from the eighteenth-century house. The room is hung with its original early-eighteenth-century Chinese wallpaper.*

Right: *Lord Harrowby's study. The library table was almost certainly made by Chippendale for the 1st Baron Harrowby.*

LORD SANDON

By the end of 1849 Burn had presented five different schemes. It was not until May 1850 that there was sufficient agreement for a design to be put out to tender, and then the estimates came back higher than Burn had led the Harrowbys to expect: '*all the fat is in the fire* as I expected', wrote Lady Harrowby to her second son. 'We shall have to begin again de novo.' She was right, and the foundation stone was not laid until January 1852. That was not the end of the problems, as the Harrowbys demanded changes to the design while the house was being built. Much against his better judgement, Burn agreed for reasons of economy to drop the proposed projecting centrepiece on the garden front, leaving it a flat expanse of windows. When the Harrowbys insisted on changes to the windows in the entrance hall, Burn – always a blunt-spoken man – resigned. He was temporarily pacified, but then in effect walked out again when his design for the entrance hall floor was set aside. He agreed to return only to check the accounts. It was not until June 1855 – seven years after the fire – that the Harrowbys finally left the inn in the village and moved into Sandon Hall.

Despite all this unhappiness – commemorated by the family in the name they gave to their WC, 'Wm Burn' – there is nothing about Sandon to suggest any departure from Burn's normal practices. It is unremarkably Jacobean in style, with the attractive addition of Scottish strapwork ornament around the windows and porch. The detailing of the interior woodwork and plasterwork is simple. As Burn's assistant, William B. Colling, told Lord Harrowby, the details were taken from a recent, familiar source, Joseph Nash's *Mansions of England in the Olden Time* (1849). Sandon is one of the very few houses by Burn where it is still possible to see how the architectural framework was designed to allow textiles, wallpapers and furniture to be displayed to advantage. In plan, Burn adopted his usual division between the reception rooms and a private family wing, separated here by the main staircase. The reception rooms are arranged as two enfilades: on the north side, the staircase and the hall, divided into three by screens of columns; to their south, overlooking the garden, the dining room, drawing room and library.

There is a long account of Sandon shortly after it was finished by Cecylia Dzialynska, a Polish visitor, who came for luncheon in 1858. After passing between two lines of servants in white and red livery, she was taking off her coat when 'Lord Harrowby came running in, small, thin, grey, wearing glasses, with the most hearty welcome in the world.' She was impressed by everything in the house, from the stairs, 'smooth like a mirror', to the kitchen and cellars – 'how everything there shines, nobody will believe who did not see it.' That she was given this comprehensive tour suggests that the family, despite the troubled building history, was more than pleased with Sandon Hall. It remains a seat of the Earls of Harrowby.

The library. Its bookcases were made by a London firm, George Trollope & Sons, who also supplied carpets, curtains and picture frames for the house.

FLINTHAM HALL, NOTTINGHAMSHIRE

A very few Victorian houses are so intact that they deserve to be preserved as carefully as a fragile ancient woodland or an orchid meadow. Flintham Hall has survived into the twenty-first century with astonishing completeness; there is hardly anywhere else in England that so authentically evokes the confidence of the landed classes in the 1850s and the comfort of their lives.

In 1789 the Thorotons, an old-established Nottinghamshire gentry family, extended their landholdings with the purchase of the Flintham estate, about 15 miles south of Newark. Flintham Hall, which has medieval origins, was then largely seventeenth-century in appearance. Following an advantageous marriage in 1815, the family added the name Hildyard to their own, and in 1829 commissioned Lewis Wyatt to extend and reface the house, creating a stuccoed Classical building.

Above: *Flintham Hall from the drive, photographed in 1979. The turreted tower rising over the* porte-cochère *was part of the additions designed by T. C. Hine and built in 1853–57.*

Left: *The library, always used as the principal living room, occupies the wing added in the 1850s. The conservatory is visible through the windows at the far end.*

In 1853 Thomas Blackborne Thoroton Hildyard MP decided to remodel it again. His motives are not clear, as he was neither young nor rich (his estates were mortgaged) and he had recently separated from his wife. He seems to have been naturally extravagant: in 1848 he bought a large house in Eaton Square in London, which he had expensively furnished by Holland & Sons. In their shop he saw a huge chimneypiece-cum-bookcase, designed by T. R. Macquoid in Italian Cinquecento style, that Holland had made for display at the Great Exhibition of 1851. Hildyard bought it in 1852 for £500, but had nowhere to put it. Within months he was consulting the Nottingham architect T. C. Hine about remodelling Flintham.

Hine had established his reputation with the design of Nottingham's Corn Exchange in 1849. One of the city's most successful Victorian architects, he worked in free Italianate and Elizabethan styles, which he layered onto buildings that were usually Classical in basic disposition. He was a natural choice for Hildyard, who seems at first to have contemplated simply encasing the existing house with stone, adding a conservatory and lodges and extending the

service accommodation. Yet he almost doubled his budget for the house as work progressed, from the £7,359 that was originally estimated to the £14,480 that he actually spent. The additional expense had been incurred by the decision to raise a turreted tower over the *porte-cochère*, and to extend the house with not only a conservatory but also a two-storey library wing.

Hildyard was not bookish, and his new double-height, galleried library was not conceived as a place for study. It has always been the principal living room, a glorious, spacious surprise after the relatively low rooms that precede it. Screens of columns, galleries and bays create a complex space that demand leisurely exploration. The room seems never to have been repainted since the decorator James Marshall finished work here in the autumn of 1857. The fireplace's green Mona marble is picked up in the green walls and curtains; its red marble is echoed in the columns and stencilled decoration.

At the far end of the room, windows look into the house's most remarkable survival, the conservatory. At gallery level, the windows slide back so that people sitting in the library can hear the splashing of the conservatory's fountain, or walk out onto a Venetian balcony that looks down into its luxuriant planting, lit by gas jets modelled in porcelain as Dorothea lilies – they also were shown at the Great Exhibition. Rising higher than the main body of the house, the conservatory's barrel-vaulted, glazed roof recalls the Crystal Palace, but only the roof is iron-framed; its projecting walls are glazed stone screens imitating iron. Externally, these help to integrate the conservatory into the heavy, early-seventeenth-century Classical ornament of Hine's new wing and recasing of the old house.

The work nearly bankrupted Hildyard, and in 1885 the estate was offered for sale, but no buyer could be found. Fortunately, Hildyard's heir married a rich woman, and the family was able to pay off its debts. For much of the twentieth century Flintham was owned by Hildyard's great-grandson, Myles Thoroton Hildyard, described in *The Times* obituary as 'a man of letters and a resourceful soldier', who 'loved his house, his garden, his paintings and handsome young men.' When he died in 2005, at the age of ninety, he had lived at Flintham for seventy-seven years. He bequeathed the house to his nephew and it remains a private family home.

Above: *The house from the garden. In the foreground is the remodelled Regency house; Hine's library wing and conservatory extend beyond.*

Right: *The conservatory: a rare survivor of a fashionable feature in mid-nineteenth-century country houses.*

MILTON ERNEST HALL, BEDFORDSHIRE

In 1848 and 1850 there were major gold rushes, first in California and then in Australia. In England, some businessmen were apprehensive about the financial effects of these discoveries. Among them was Benjamin Helps Starey, whose family were prosperous linen drapers in London. The likelihood of a dramatic increase in the world supply of gold prompted Starey, then in his early forties, to diversify his assets by investing in land as a hedge against inflation. He decided to move his family from Reigate to Milton Ernest, a few miles north of Bedford, where in 1853 he bought an estate of 590 acres for £22,000. In his diary, he recorded visiting his new acquisition with his architect: 'The house thoroughly bad irreparable: and it was decided to build a good family residence which the plans for were then put in hand and in February 1854 we began to take down the old house and stack away the materials.' In July 1858 the new house was ready for the family to move in.

Starey's architect was his brother-in-law, William Butterfield. Milton Ernest Hall is of exceptional interest as the sole commission for a new country house by one of the greatest Gothic designers of the nineteenth century. In the 1850s Butterfield was a leader of a generation determined to show that Gothic could be a style to suit all modern needs. They believed that architects should study medieval precedents not to imitate them but to synthesize them into a new, contemporary style – Gothic developed, not Gothic revived. Drawing on a wide range of precedents, including North European and Italian medieval architecture, they introduced sculpture and coloured materials into their buildings wherever possible, partly as a

Above: *The garden front. At ground-floor level, the triple-height bay window lights the library. Unusually, the servants' hall, on the far left, was given a garden view.*

Left: *The approach to Milton Ernest Hall. The east front, visible here, is the most austere of the house's complex, varied façades.*

reaction against the austere Neo-Classicism or skimpy Tudor of the preceding generation.

The style that resulted, now known as 'High Victorian', is closely associated with ecclesiastical design, and Butterfield was essentially an architect of churches, convents and parsonages. He was responsible for the building that pioneered the High Victorian movement, All Saints, Margaret Street, London, begun in 1851. Although a comparably ambitious exercise in 'developed' Gothic, Milton Ernest Hall reveals a less familiar aspect of his career. Butterfield was devoted to his sister's family, who shared his High Church piety, and took great pleasure in designing a home for them where he – a lifelong bachelor – would always be welcome.

Forcefully Gothic although it is, the house does not look like any medieval building. Its boldly modelled forms, pulled together by the high roof, are determined by its plan: Butterfield strongly believed that form followed function. His eschewal of medievalism is shown in the small-paned sash windows that he always preferred for domestic buildings, and the simple, almost Regency furniture that he designed for the house, some of it painted in gay stripes that echo the subtle polychromy of the exterior, in which brick and stone are chequered and striped. The house is part of a larger programme of work by Butterfield at Milton Ernest that included farm buildings, a boat house in the garden – which is bordered by the River Ouse – a mill and mill house, several cottages and the restoration of the parish church, all paid for by the Stareys.

They were not able to enjoy their new home for long. In 1872, losses on the stock exchange forced Benjamin Starey to sell the estate for less than a third of what he had laid out on it. His health never recovered from the shock, and he died only two years later. However, his younger son, John, a tea and rubber planter first in Ceylon and then Malaya, amassed a sufficient fortune to buy the estate back in 1919. The house was sold again in 1968. As a result the interiors were never adequately recorded while still in domestic use. The house was semi-derelict when Alex Starkey photographed it so beautifully for an article by Mark Girouard in *Country Life* in 1969. After various vicissitudes, including a short period as a hotel, the house became a care home for the elderly.

Above: *The entrance front, viewed from the farmyard opposite the house. The close proximity of the Stareys' farm to their new house suggests an indifference to the usual Victorian determination to keep the working parts of an estate out of sight.*

Right: *The service wing, photographed from the bank of the River Ouse. The line of buttresses was designed to reinforce a water tank.*

OMNIA VINCIT AMOR ET NOS CEDAMUS AMORI

1860

LORDS OF CREATION

Victorian power and prosperity reached their zenith in the 1860s. Britain was incontestably the richest nation on the globe and, in a decade when the USA was rent by civil war, it was also the only country with world-power status. It was equally a period when the country's old and new economies seemed to be in equilibrium. Agriculture, far from suffering from the abolition of tariffs in the 1840s, had – thanks to landowners' investment in new techniques and technology – entered a golden age, well equipped to supply the enormous domestic market created by urbanization and industrialization. That sense of confidence is evident in the houses built or begun during the 1860s, yet even a cursory examination of the sources of the wealth which created them reveals that they are far from being simply the product of well-managed agricultural estates.

There is no doubt that many estate owners spent very great sums on improvements, yet even in the 1860s the rewards were meagre by the standards of the manufacturing and financial industries. Most landowners were satisfied with a return of two or two-and-a-half per cent in a decade when bank interest rates were usually between three-and-a-half per cent and four-and-a-half per cent. In other words, well before the agricultural depression which began in the late 1870s, land was a luxury. Yet it was attractive to an industrialist, banker or merchant who wished for the social status that estate ownership unquestionably bestowed, summed up by *The Economist* in 1867 as 'the sherrifalty, a squeeze of the hand from the Lord Lieutenant, the county balls for his wife and daughters, and perhaps an opening to the House of Commons.' And, as well as providing sport and other amenities, land offered the pleasure of architectural patronage.

It was already unlikely that any new house on a grand scale would be paid for entirely out of the revenues of an agricultural estate. Even a traditional aristocrat such as Earl Manvers relied to a considerable degree on revenue from coal mines when replacing his family seat at Thoresby. Brodsworth was paid for by a banking fortune and Bishops Court was transformed by City mercantile money. The Marquess of Bute owned large estates in Scotland and Wales, but it was the enormous enlargement of the ground rents from his Cardiff properties, following the transformation of the city into a great port, which paid for the dazzling medieval fantasies designed for him by William Burges. Although equally pious and high-minded, William Gibbs was in most ways very different from Lord Bute, but even this tough businessman clearly derived great enjoyment from ambitious architectural patronage. Historians' customary emphasis on the way that such men as Gibbs purchased status by investing in country houses neglects the exuberant pleasure in artistic creation that buildings such as Tyntesfield abundantly reveal.

1870

The Winter Smoking Room at Cardiff Castle, Glamorganshire, designed by William Burges and begun in 1869.

BISHOPS COURT, DEVON

On 12 June 1863 the chapel at Bishops Court was consecrated by the Bishop of Exeter, an appropriate climax to the remodelling of the house over the previous four years. Its owner, John Garratt, had set out to revive not only architecturally, but also spiritually, a building that in medieval times had belonged to the Church.

Four miles east of Exeter, Bishops Court was the principal summer palace of the bishops until 1550, when it was expropriated by the Crown. In 1800 it was bought by Lord Graves, a distinguished admiral. His son demolished the great hall to create a symmetrical, pedimented entrance front, stuccoed the walls and inserted sash windows with Gothic glazing bars.

In 1833 the estate was sold to John Garratt, senior partner in a London firm of tea and coffee merchants, who had decided to retire to the country. Garratt was rich – in 1809 his father's estate was valued for probate at £400,000 – and determined to spend his money responsibly. He improved the house with new lodges and an ornamental lake, and provided a new church and school for Sowton, the estate village. Then, in 1846, he suffered a stroke, and handed Bishops Court over to his son, John.

Every bit as serious-minded as his father, John Garratt Jr had a strong interest in ecclesiastical architecture, fostered by his High Church beliefs. His new house was everything the mid-Victorians hated – neat, plain and, in its use of stucco to conceal masonry, sham. To Garratt, moreover, the conversion of a bishop's palace to secular use, its chapel surviving but redundant, symbolized the decline of the ideals of the medieval church. The restoration of the house that followed his father's death in 1859 was not merely an aesthetic imperative – it was a religious duty.

Garratt was well equipped to oversee the work. In 1841 he had become a founder member of the Exeter Diocesan Architectural Society and took a close interest in local church restoration and

Above: *The west front. The pair of buttresses marks the chapel.*

Left: *The staircase, photographed in 1989. William White's love of colour appears extravagantly in the massive (but structurally unnecessary) marble columns, which are crowned by beautiful foliage carving.*

building. He chose as his architect William White, a fellow member of the society. Like William Butterfield, White was determined to show that Gothic could be developed from its medieval origins to serve the needs of the nineteenth century. Bishops Court is as much a showpiece of modern Gothic as Milton Ernest Hall (see pages 70–73).

White believed that architects had lost the medieval ability to fuse a variety of elements into a harmonious unity. Bishops Court exemplifies his ideals: the picturesquely irregular parts are kept tightly subordinate to the whole. This is especially evident in the garden front, where the long, level cornice powerfully embodies one of White's guiding principles for design – horizontality. As he wrote in 1851, 'a long line of roof or wall is almost the only way of relieving the otherwise monotonous effect of a *mass* of broken forms.'

White's beliefs about architectural design are exemplified in the exterior's most conspicuous feature, colour. For White, monochrome architecture was a psychological deprivation. Like many of his contemporaries, he wanted 'structural polychromy' – colour from materials rather than paint – but he criticized the busy striping and diapering evident in some 1850s buildings; he preferred 'diffusion' of colour. This is precisely what he achieved in the exterior of Bishops Court, where the red-brown Heavitree masonry is flecked and stippled with coloured stones. Colour is equally evident inside, where, miraculously, White's painted decorative schemes have survived. The all-over geometrical stencil patterns on a buff ground, which reach their climax in the restored chapel, are the setting for inventive Gothic chimneypieces and highly original Gothic furniture.

The house remained in the Garratt family until 1956, when it was sold, with most of its contents, to G. C. Taylor, who preserved it intact as the headquarters of his family paint business. After his death, the house was sold and its contents dispersed at auction in 1994.

Right: *The entrance hall and main corridor, separated by a Gothic arcade. White's stencilled decoration survives intact. At the far end of the corridor painted angels appear over the door to the chapel* (above).

BRODSWORTH HALL, YORKSHIRE

Whether Gothic, like Tyntesfield, or Jacobean, like Thoresby, the style of many large new country houses built or rebuilt in the 1860s reveals a desire to emphasize their place in the long history of Britain's landed classes. Yet a substantial number of estate owners also continued to commission Classical designs. There is little evidence about their motives for what was in some ways an old-fashioned choice. Was it simply comfort and convenience? Tantalisingly, given how completely the house survives, we know nothing about Charles Sabine Thellusson's reasons for deciding to rebuild the eighteenth-century house at Brodsworth in a Classical manner, nor is it evident why he chose an Italian architect. Although opulently fitted out, the house is restrained in its architectural forms, with none of the picturesque asymmetry that Charles Barry, for example, would have sought. There is not even a tower.

Thellusson grew up with expectations of enormous wealth compromised by bitter family disputes which by 1859, when he finally came into his inheritance, had lasted for over sixty years. The source of the money that paid for the new Brodsworth Hall was his great-grandfather Peter Thellusson, a member of a Huguenot banking family. When he died in 1797, having made a fortune in finance and in trade with the West Indies, he left most of his money – estimated at between £600,000 and £800,000 – in trust to accumulate during the lifetimes of his sons and grandsons. When the last died, the fund was to be distributed amongst all his 'eldest male lineal descendants'. The will caused a sensation: it was estimated that his eventual heirs stood to inherit £35 million. In fact, thanks to the prolonged litigation that immediately ensued, by the time that Thellusson's last grandson died, in 1856, the fortune amounted to no more than the original bequest.

However, since the House of Lords decided in 1859 that there were only two legitimate claimants to it, one of whom was Charles Sabine Thellusson, owner of Brodsworth, he was left with ample funds to rebuild the house and enjoy a life of ease. His income from the

Above: *The garden front of Brodsworth Hall, photographed in 1963.*

Right: *The staircase hall. The sculpture in the foreground, showing a young child being taught to pray, is by Giuseppe Lazzerini.*

COUNTRY LIFE

bequest, some £17,000 a year, was supplemented by a profitable coal mine on the estate, which lies seven miles north west of Doncaster. As the house was designed by an Italian, the wholly obscure Chevalier Casentini of Lucca, who also supplied the garden statuary, and is filled with marble statues by contemporary Italian sculptors, Thellusson presumably had spent time in Italy, but little is known about his travels. The construction of the house was overseen by a minor London architect, Philip Wilkinson, from 1861 to 1863.

One possible reason for Thellusson's choice of a Classical style is that it made it easier to integrate fittings from the old house into the new: many of Brodsworth's chimneypieces and doors are eighteenth-century in date. The house's Italianate flavour is most evident in the spacious series of halls, designed to display sculpture supplied by Casentini. The gleaming whiteness of these figures is wonderfully offset by the marble columns and red and ochre marbling of the walls. The crimson and gilt drawing room, however, combines Italianate painted decoration on the ceilings with French *dix-huitième* décor and furnishings, supplied by the decorators and upholsterers Lapworth Brothers of 22 Old Bond Street, London. All still survive, together with such wholly English interiors as the billiard room, complete with leather-upholstered viewing benches.

Partly because it was used only for shooting parties in the first part of the twentieth century, Brodsworth Hall survived with an intactness that a century after it was completed seemed little short of miraculous. The house was first given publicity by Mark Girouard in two articles in *Country Life* in 1963, where he wrote, 'I know of no house that recalls the flavour of one particular decade with such intensity as Brodsworth. The 1860s have been miraculously preserved in the amber richness of its rooms; extraordinarily little has been altered since it was built and furnished.' These words were to be of great importance in mustering public support for Brodsworth's preservation when, in 1990, its last private owner, Pamela Williams, offered the house to the nation. Following a grant from the National Heritage Memorial Fund for the purchase of the contents, Brodsworth passed to English Heritage, which has sought in its conservation of the interiors to preserve the atmosphere so memorably described by Mark Girouard.

Above: *The billiard room, hung with a group of equestrian pictures by James Ward.*

Left: *The drawing room. The crimson silk wall-hangings were supplied, like the furnishings, by a London firm of decorators, Lapworth Brothers. They also made the Axminster carpet especially for the room.*

THORESBY HALL, NOTTINGHAMSHIRE

Anthony Salvin's career as a country-house architect had been launched with Harlaxton Manor. Nearly thirty-five years later, it concluded with a building on a comparable scale that redeployed and refined many of the lessons that he had learned when designing his prodigy house for Gregory Gregory. At Thoresby Hall, however, his patron could hardly have been more different – the 3rd Earl Manvers was an aristocrat with very deep pockets who seems to have been happy to let his architect direct the project without interference.

Thoresby is one of a string of great estates carved out of Sherwood Forest that were known in the nineteenth century as the Dukeries – Worksop, Welbeck, Clumber and Kiveton were the others. The Pierrepont family had indeed been dukes – of Kingston-upon-Hull – but the title had become extinct by the nineteenth century. Salvin's house was the third at Thoresby. The park was enclosed, and its house rebuilt in the 1680s. This was burnt in 1745 and replaced twenty years later by a house by John Carr of York, demolished in the 1860s. Neither of these buildings provided a precedent for the vast scale of the building that Salvin designed, which reflects the enormous wealth that the family had come to enjoy. By the 1880s, the 3rd Earl Manvers had an income of over £50,000 a year from agriculture, but it seems likely that it was the revenues from his Derbyshire coal mines that accounted for his apparent indifference to cost when building Thoresby.

Lord Manvers most probably chose Salvin as his architect on the recommendation of a close friend, Ralph Sneyd, owner of Keele Hall, Staffordshire. Sneyd, an immensely rich bachelor, had commissioned Salvin to rebuild his house between 1854 and 1860, and from the beginning of work at Thoresby wrote regularly to Lord Manvers offering advice and criticism of Salvin's designs. He seems also to have recommended the great garden designer William Andrews Nesfield, Salvin's brother-in-law, who had laid out an arboretum at Keele. However, Nesfield failed to impress Lord Manvers, who asked Salvin to undertake the garden as well.

No such friction is recorded between the architect and his client, who accepted Salvin's first proposals with only modifications to the staircase tower. Work began in May 1864. In its fluent and picturesque weaving together of precedents from the most admired mansions of Tudor and Jacobean England, Thoresby is an old-fashioned house: the clock tower over the entrance is derived from Hatfield, details from Burghley are fused with ideas from Audley End, and Salvin's first proposals for the staircase tower recalled Wollaton. There is no clue here that the Gothic Revival was undergoing a period of exceptional creativity, nor is there any glimpse of the taste for the English vernacular styles that so appealed to the pupils in Salvin's

The south front of Thoresby Hall, which overlooks the garden, photographed in 1979. The clock tower over the entrance is visible on the right.

The view from the main staircase (above) *back into the great hall. The immediate model for the screen* (right) *separating the hall from the stairs is the hall at Audley End, but the way that Salvin pierced the walls to allow glimpses into the rooms also suggests Baroque influence.*

office, such as Richard Norman Shaw or Nesfield's son, William Eden Nesfield. Yet the way that Salvin composed the house's massive bulk – the south front is 182 feet long – is impressive. Forms balance, but symmetry is avoided; ornament is used sparingly, and Salvin effectively exploited the contrast between the house's rough-cut stone walls and smoothly finished dressings. This sense of tight control extends to the internal plan, which is both highly practical and almost flamboyantly theatrical.

One of the most successful aspects of Harlaxton is the way that the house is set into a slope so that the main rooms, on the *piano nobile*, open directly onto the garden. Salvin repeated the idea several times, but perhaps nowhere so memorably as at Thoresby, where, since the ground slopes much more than at Harlaxton, the site had to be excavated to the depth of a storey on the entrance front. This allowed Salvin to contrive a dramatic approach to the reception rooms that eclipses even Harlaxton's. The visitor enters at ground level a low, dark hall from which stairs ascend to the unexpected vision of the great hall. Sixty-four feet long, this mighty room rises through three storeys to its hammerbeam roof. At the far end, a wide, high arch opens onto the grand staircase. In an almost Baroque way, Salvin pierced the walls with a balcony over the staircase and arcades opening into the bedroom corridors. Sneyd had suggested this idea to Lord Manvers, after Salvin had shown him the first design.

The great hall has a practical purpose (beyond the entertainment of the Pierreponts' tenantry) as it is the house's main circulation space, providing easy access to the principal reception rooms. For a house on this scale, Thoresby has surprisingly few rooms for entertaining – a drawing room, library, breakfast room and dining room arranged *en filade* along the south front – but this is explained by their palatial scale, as each is a double-height room. Their decoration fuses Jacobean ornament with French eighteenth-century motifs. This was hardly an original idea by the 1860s, but at Thoresby it had a particular point as Lord Manvers's wife, Georgine, was half-French, the daughter (and co-heir) of the duc de Coigny and an English mother. The French furniture and chandeliers visible in *Country Life*'s photographs of the drawing room were inherited by her from the Château de Coigny.

Thoresby was completed in 1873, having cost £171,000. Lord Manvers was clearly pleased with it, for he immediately commissioned Salvin to design stables and a riding school (which alone, at nearly £28,000, cost more than most country houses) and an estate church at Perlethorpe. Thoresby survived as a fully staffed country house until the death of the 6th, and last, Earl Manvers in 1955. His widow continued to live there until she died in 1984. A proposal to undermine the house led the Coal Board to buy it to forestall compensation claims for subsidence. The family retained part of the contents and have built a new Palladian house on the estate, out of sight of the old Thoresby Hall, which is now a hotel.

The drawing room. Salvin's plasterwork incorporates Rococo motifs to complement the French eighteenth-century furniture inherited by Countess Manvers.

CARDIFF CASTLE, GLAMORGANSHIRE

In 1865 the greatest builder of country houses in nineteenth-century Britain met the architect of his dreams. John Patrick Crichton-Stuart, 3rd Marquess of Bute, was barely eighteen, and still an undergraduate at Oxford, when he entrusted William Burges with the project that would crown the architect's career: the rebuilding of Cardiff Castle. Burges began work by making a survey of the ruins of the Norman castle, reconstructed in the fifteenth century by Richard Beauchamp, Earl of Warwick. Its only habitable parts were the lodgings rebuilt in 1777–78 by Henry Holland in a tame Gothic fashion for Lord Bute's grandfather. Burges's report proposed three possible approaches: maintain the buildings as a ruin, restore them to their medieval appearance, or take the opportunity to incorporate them into a new house. Burges favoured the third idea: 'We must never lose sight of the fact that Cardiff Castle is not an antiquarian ruin but the seat of the Marquis of Bute.' Lord Bute enthusiastically agreed, but he had to wait until 1868, when he came of age, before he could begin work.

On achieving his majority, Lord Bute came into one of the greatest fortunes of the century. His family owned extensive estates in Scotland, but the source of the wealth that was to be used to transform Cardiff Castle was the city of Cardiff itself. In the early nineteenth century his father had invested virtually all the family's financial resources in the creation of the Cardiff Docks, which turned a town of barely 1,000 inhabitants into one of the world's major ports, the principal outlet from which Welsh iron and coal flowed out to the industrializing world. The 2nd Marquess died in 1848, when his son was only six months old, and the building of the docks was completed in 1859 by his trustees. The infant inherited an income of £300,000 a year.

Above: *Cardiff Castle seen from Bute Park. The clock tower, completed in 1873, is on the far right, the octagonal, fifteenth-century Beauchamp Tower in the centre.*

Left: *The Octagon Stairs in the Beauchamp Tower, photographed in 1961. The marble heraldic lion at the foot of the stair rail alludes to the Butes' royal Stuart ancestry; its closed visor indicates that they are of illegitimate descent.*

What shulde I seyn
Men myghte in that
Benyngly
By hir
goddesse of Nature
ymned or hys make
Lucretia
Dido
mon joly
cuer est

Lord Bute's introduction to his architect resulted from Burges's father, Alfred, a marine engineer, having worked on the construction of the docks. Superficially, architect and patron were very different. Taciturn and austere, with a strong sense of the responsibilities of his station, Lord Bute had a questing religious nature which led him to convert to Roman Catholicism when he was twenty-one, an event that provided the plot for Disraeli's novel *Lothair* (1870). Burges, for all that he was a leader in the movement to create a modern Gothic style, had little or no interest in religion. He was short, bald, jocular and bohemian, at ease with artists and actors. Yet both he and Lord Bute were in love with a vision of the Middle Ages as an alternative to, or escape from, the modern world, and for both men this ideal had deep scholarly foundations. Lord Bute was an accomplished linguist and liturgiologist, who published numerous books, including a translation of the Breviary. Burges's knowledge of his favoured models, the early-thirteenth-century Gothic buildings of France and England, was profound, and he added to it a close study of Classical, Arabic and Islamic architecture and design: sources of inspiration that are evident in his work for the 3rd Marquess.

By 1867 Burges had formulated his design for his first addition to the castle – the element that the building most evidently lacked, a mighty tower. The foundations of the clock tower were laid in 1869. When begun, Lord Bute was still unmarried, so the tower was conceived of as a bachelor suite, with a bedroom, dressing room, a winter smoking room at its base and a summer smoking room at the top. Its interiors, and those that followed in the next decade, are some of the most magnificent that the Gothic Revival ever achieved: complex fusions of painting, sculpture, tiles and stained glass illustrating themes of great iconographical intricacy drawn from literature, history and astrology.

Above: *The 3rd Marquess of Bute's bedroom. The ceiling beams are inscribed 'John' – Lord Bute's first name – spelled out in Greek letters. On the green marble chimneyhood is a metal figure of St John the Evangelist. The bedcover was designed by William Burges.*

Left: *The Chaucer Room, created by William Burges for the Marchioness of Bute, at the top of the Beauchamp Tower. A figure of Chaucer, carved by Thomas Nicholl, presides over the chimneypiece; above the oak panelling (which is inlaid with mother-of-pearl) are paintings of characters from Chaucer's* Legend of Good Women. *The room's tiled floor is conceived of as a vine-leaf maze.*

By the time that the clock tower was finished in 1873, Lord Bute had married Gwendolen Fitzalan-Howard, a daughter of Lord Howard of Glossop, and so the rest of the castle was planned for family use. 'Pray don't imagine my dear', wrote Lord Bute to his future wife in 1872, 'that the house is all done up as if we were living in the reign of Henry III. There is only my sitting room, the oratory and the new tower. The rest is by no means satisfactory, and has been the victim of every barbarism since the Renaissance.' Although the arrangement of rooms in towers is unusual, in plan Cardiff Castle is not very different from a normal Victorian country house. The Butes needed private suites for themselves and rooms for their children and for guests. Large reception rooms were required, partly so that Lord Bute could fulfil his civic duties in Cardiff. Even so, the castle was not Lord Bute's principal seat – that was Mount Stuart on the Isle of Bute – and he and his family spent only two months a year in Cardiff; consequently, it was never quite a conventional family home. Moreover, it was built in a very leisurely way: it was far from finished when Burges died in 1881 and major elements were still incomplete when Lord Bute died in 1900, thirty-two years after work had begun.

An architectural patron whose primarily interest was the process of design and building, the 3rd Marquess of Bute embarked on dozens of new buildings and restorations of old ones. In Wales alone, he commissioned Burges to restore Castell Coch, a small medieval castle a few miles outside Cardiff; he paid for the excavation of Cardiff's Greyfriars church and the site of the thirteenth-century Blackfriars monastery, discovered at the edge of Cardiff Castle's grounds; and in the 1880s he began work on restoring Caerphilly, the largest castle in Wales. Lord Bute once remarked to the architect Robert Rowand Anderson, who worked for him at Mount Stuart, 'Why should I hurry over what is my chief pleasure? I have comparatively little interest in a thing after it is finished.' This helps to explain why the interiors of Cardiff Castle were conceived of largely as works of art, divorced from the requirements of daily life.

In 1947 Lord Bute's grandson, the 5th Marquess, presented Cardiff Castle and the adjacent park to Cardiff City Corporation. The Corporation acquired at the same time part of its contents, so that the rooms could remain furnished. The long tradition of public opening was continued, but at a time when interest in Victorian art and architecture was at its nadir, the castle was regarded not as an historic house, but primarily as a suitable backdrop for civic functions. In the past twenty years that has changed. Burges's decorative schemes are being conserved, and furniture that left the castle in the twentieth century is being bought back when it comes on to the market. Loans from the Bute family of textiles, such as curtains, wall-hangings and bedcovers, mostly designed by Burges, are helping also to give a much fuller sense of the original appearance of these extraordinary interiors.

The banqueting hall, the largest room in the castle, and its principal reception room. The design of the roof draws on fifteenth-century East Anglian precedents. Its murals, based on cartoons by H. W. Londsdale, and the chimneypiece by Nicholl depict scenes from the Norman history of Glamorganshire.

MADRESFIELD, WORCESTERSHIRE

Thanks to its idyllic setting on a moated site in the shadow of the Malvern Hills, and its fame as one of the models for Brideshead in Evelyn Waugh's novel, Madresfield exerts a romantic fascination. Historically, this is amply deserved. The house and estate have passed solely by inheritance since the twelfth century; the Lygon family has been seated here since 1450. From the far side of its moat, the house's gables and towers cluster around a tall, spired bell turret with delicately picturesque effect. In summer the scent of the rose garden permeates the house and floats across the moat. Is the aura of ancient romance spoiled by the information that, in visual terms, virtually all the house is a Victorian creation?

Above: *The entrance front. The Tudor block on the right was raised by a storey in the Victorian rebuilding. The tall bell turret was erected in 1875, to mark the completion of the external works.*

Left: *The inner courtyard at Madresfield, photographed in 1907. Designed by P. C. Hardwick, it is entirely a creation of the 1860s.*

Having lived in relatively modest obscurity at Madresfield for three hundred and fifty years, the Lygons began to play a larger role in national political life at the end of the eighteenth century. In 1806 William Lygon was given a barony and in 1815 was created Earl Beauchamp. His social ambitions prompted changes to Madresfield. No major additions had been made to the higgeldy-piggeldy medieval and Elizabethan courtyard house for two centuries when, in 1799, he commissioned the architect George Byfield to design a substantial Georgian wing on the north side of the house, and remodel the other interiors. So thoroughly did Byfield do his work that when Mary Yorke visited in 1810 she asked Lord Beauchamp 'to trace out to me the old house, which he did with some difficulty, one room being left in its former state.'

The juxtaposition of an ancient house with a modern extension usually proved intolerable to Victorian eyes, and Madresfield was no different: in 1863 the 5th Earl Beauchamp commissioned a complete

remodelling, designed to bring the house back into stylistic unity and to give the plan some semblance of convenience. His architect was P. C. Hardwick, who was then working on the church and almshouses at Newland, Worcestershire, founded as the result of a bequest by the 3rd Earl Beauchamp, who had died in 1853. Hardwick's mixture of Gothic for the church and Tudor for the almshouses is very successful and presumably prompted the Earl's invitation to work at Madresfield.

The grandson and son of architects, Hardwick is probably best remembered today for his French-inspired commercial work, notably the Great Western Hotel at Paddington Station, London, built in 1851–53. Yet with his father, Philip, he had helped to design some of the finest Tudor Revival buildings in the nineteenth century, the new hall and library at Lincoln's Inn, London, completed in 1845, and he could work with fluency and authority in Gothic, as his design for Charterhouse School in Surrey, opened in 1872, reveals. He certainly had the knowledge and experience to tackle Madresfield.

Hardwick drew up his designs in 1863–64, originally with the intention of retaining as much of the old house as possible, but as the 6th Earl later commented, 'on examination it was found necessary, for the most part, to substitute reconstruction for repair.' The Tudor entrance tower was preserved but raised by an extra storey, and the courtyard in the centre of the house was opened up and given a glass roof (removed in 1887). Byfield's extension was replaced by a new wing, containing a drawing room, book room and bedrooms. The medieval great hall was rebuilt and fitted out with seventeenth-century panelling from a farmhouse at Newland. The west wing, between the courtyard and the garden, was rebuilt on the old foundations, preserving the form of its Elizabethan first-floor gallery, to

Above: *The dining room, an 1863 reconstruction of the medieval great hall, photographed in 1980.*

Right: *The staircase hall, at the centre of Hardwick's north wing. It was fitted out for the 7th Earl Beauchamp in the early twentieth century.*

which a bay window was added. On its ground floor is a smoking room and library, which opens into Hardwick's major addition to the house: a small Gothic chapel.

In the confined space into which Madresfield is squeezed, Hardwick contrived a remarkable – almost overwhelming – variety. His stylistic detail is far from predictable. Most delightful of all is the half-timbered inner courtyard, with an open gallery running along its west side. It is a composition that evokes a stage set for *Die Meistersinger von Nürnberg* – premiered in 1868 – especially as the beams are infilled with plaster panels decorated with sgraffito in an almost Germanic way. The intricately leaded lights on the west and south sides contrast engagingly with the big Perpendicular windows of the hall on the north; the final touch in this decorative display is the pavement, laid out as a maze, added in 1888.

In 1866, only two years after work had begun, the 5th Earl died of tuberculosis, and the project was taken over by his younger brother, Frederick, the 6th Earl. His first wife having died in 1876, he married Emily Pierrepont, eldest daughter of the 3rd Earl Manvers, who had recently completed Salvin's new Thoresby Hall in Nottinghamshire. Her mother was half-French, which probably explains why she chose to furnish her bedroom and a drawing room in Second Empire style.

It seems that work proceeded slowly, for when the 6th Earl died in 1891, a year after Hardwick, the staircase hall at the centre of the north block had not been completed. As it now exists this is largely an Edwardian creation and is often said to consist of the knocking together of two or more of Hardwick's rooms. In plan, however, it existed in its present form by 1898, and may owe its narrow, high proportions simply to the requirement laid on Hardwick to stick to the foundations of the old house. The 7th Earl and his wife, whose patronage of the Arts and Crafts movement falls outside the chronological scope of this book, commissioned new fittings for the library from C. R. Ashbee and had the chapel decorated by artists and craftsmen from the Birmingham Group. They consulted both Randall Wells and Ernest Gimson about the fitting-out of the hall, top-lit by three domed skylights, but it is not clear if anyone apart from Lord Beauchamp marshalled the decorative scheme, in which the ebony woodwork is enhanced by such luxury touches as crystal newels. It has been suggested by the historian Alan Brooks that the towering Jacobean-style chimneypiece of alabaster, porphyry and serpentine may have been designed by Alfred Waterhouse, as it was a wedding gift to Lady Beauchamp in 1902 from her brother Bendor, 2nd Duke of Westminster, owner of Waterhouse's Eaton Hall. It is not, perhaps, a very happy monument, since in 1931 the Duke hounded his sister's husband into exile when he learned of his homosexual proclivities – the story which inspired Waugh in *Brideshead Revisited* to create a house whose owner is forced to live abroad.

Madresfield is now the home of Lady Rosalind Morrison, a niece of the 8th, and last, Lord Beauchamp.

Madresfield Court from the east. On the far left is the bay window of the library, from which the chapel projects.

TYNTESFIELD, SOMERSET

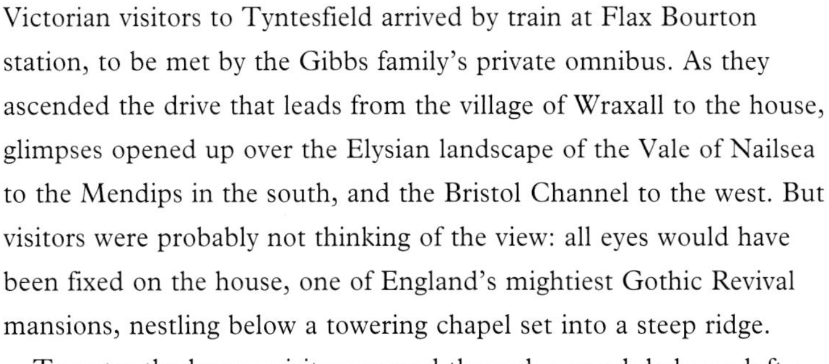

Victorian visitors to Tyntesfield arrived by train at Flax Bourton station, to be met by the Gibbs family's private omnibus. As they ascended the drive that leads from the village of Wraxall to the house, glimpses opened up over the Elysian landscape of the Vale of Nailsea to the Mendips in the south, and the Bristol Channel to the west. But visitors were probably not thinking of the view: all eyes would have been fixed on the house, one of England's mightiest Gothic Revival mansions, nestling below a towering chapel set into a steep ridge.

To enter the house, visitors passed through a porch below a lofty clock tower bristling with tourelles; if it were evening, the clock face would be illuminated by gaslight. Carved into the wall to the left of the entrance is the family coat of arms, with the motto 'I place my faith in God', a foretaste of the atmosphere within. These words are not in English, or Latin, but Spanish – '*En dios mi amparo y esperanza*'. Tyntesfield's Gothic forms proclaim not feudal longevity but modern piety, and the money with which it was built derives from sources very far from Somerset.

When he acquired Tyntesfield – then known as Tyntes Place – in 1843, the fifty-three-year-old William Gibbs was a well-established businessman. He came from a family of Devon gentry who in the eighteenth century had produced merchants of remarkable dynamism. In 1778 Antony Gibbs, William's father, set up a company to trade with Spain. When the Peninsular Wars brought that business to a halt, the firm diversified into South America, the beginning of what became a multi-national trading and banking enterprise. Antony established its headquarters in London, and on his death in 1808 Antony Gibbs & Sons was inherited by William and his brother.

In 1841 William Gibbs took an immense commercial gamble when he signed contracts worth £1 million with the Peruvian and Bolivian governments to import guano – the dried droppings of sea birds – for use as fertiliser. The first shipment arrived the following year. It was enthusiastically adopted by British farmers and Antony Gibbs & Co. made its fortune. Between 1842, when Gibbs became head of the firm, and 1875, when he died, the partners' profits averaged £80,000–£100,000 a year. By the 1860s, when he was estimated to have capital worth £1.5 million invested in the business, Gibbs was one of the richest commoners in England.

It would be interesting to know whether he bought Tyntesfield, and built up an estate for it, in part to diversify his assets. However, his principal reasons for acquiring a country house were personal. In 1839 he had married his cousin Matilda Blanche Crawley-Boevey of Flaxley Abbey, Gloucestershire, twenty-eight years his junior, and over the next decade they had seven children. She took a strong interest in the revival of sacramental and ceremonial life in the Church of England promoted by the Oxford Movement and her husband was entirely

The entrance front of Tyntesfield in 1902. The chapel's bell turret and apse are visible on the right. The large bay window to the left of the entrance lights the library.

sympathetic to her beliefs. He was a considerable patron of church restoration and building, and in 1873 gave £50,000 for the chapel of Keble College, Oxford, by William Butterfield.

Tyntesfield had been rebuilt as recently as 1836–40 as a small country house in a restrained Tudor style. It was evidently well laid out, as its principal features – the L-shaped entrance courtyard, long south front with a big central gable and picturesquely irregular west front with a conservatory at the north-west corner – were all preserved in the house that swallowed it up twenty years later. In 1854 Gibbs commissioned a refurbishment from the well-known interior decorating firm of John Gregory Crace. Based in Wigmore Street, London, Crace had a high reputation for Gothic work, thanks to his long-standing collaboration with A. W. N. Pugin. At Tyntesfield, he repainted and wallpapered almost every room, refitted the dining room and supplied new furniture, upholstered in burgundy and gold silk, some of which survives.

Gibbs was taken aback by Crace's high charges. Given his dislike of extravagance, it is especially surprising, therefore, that in 1863, when he was seventy-three, he embarked on the almost complete reconstruction of Tyntesfield. It seems likely that he was encouraged by his eldest son, Antony, who had shown no aptitude for business and had been set up as a country gentleman with a house a mile or so north of Wraxall. The realization that his heirs would be principally landowners may have prompted Gibbs to enlarge the house. His architect, John Norton, is now best remembered for Tyntesfield, but he had a busy London practice, with commissions ranging from the Winter Gardens at Great Yarmouth to a castle in Estonia. A former pupil of Benjamin Ferrey, the friend and biographer of A. W. N. Pugin, Norton worked in a competent Puginian Gothic, increasingly enlivened in the 1850s and 1860s by fashionable foreign detail. He had been born in Bristol, a connection that brought him many commissions for churches, country houses and other buildings in the area, which is probably how he came to Gibbs's notice.

Above: *The hallway, looking towards the front door. The Gothic coat stand was designed and made in 1878 by the Warwickshire cabinetmaker James Plucknett, who supplied several pieces of massive Gothic furniture for the house.*

Left: *The stair hall, which rises the full height of the house, photographed in 2002. The bust, by Lawrence Macdonald, depicts William Gibbs, for whom the house was rebuilt in the 1860s. It was carved in Rome in 1861. On the stair wall is* St Lawrence *by Juan Luis Zambarno of Córdoba, bought by Gibbs in Spain in 1853 as a Zurbarán.*

By 1865, Tyntesfield had been transformed into a great Gothic house, at a cost of some £70,000. Norton entirely refaced it in Bath stone carved with lively ornament. The central block of the south front was raised by one storey, and the mighty clock tower, its design derived from the tower over the Danube Bridge in Prague, now dominated the entrance front. The conservatory was replaced by an iron-framed domed room, 80 feet long, with a gilt-copper cupola modelled on San Marco in Venice. Inside, the rooms were fitted out with large, polychromatic Gothic chimneypieces.

This was not, however, the end of the work. In 1872 Gibbs commissioned Arthur Blomfield to add a chapel. Blomfield's model for this French-looking apsed building, lifted over a high undercroft (originally intended to serve as a family mausoleum), was ultimately the Sainte Chapelle in Paris, but it had significant Gothic Revival sources also, notably the chapel by George Gilbert Scott at Exeter College, Oxford – Antony Gibbs's old college. Beautifully decorated with mosaics by Salviati, stained glass by Powell, carving by Forsyth and metalwork by Barkentin and Krall, Tyntesfield's chapel is a perfectly preserved monument to Gibbs's munificence and piety, the visual as well as the spiritual heart of the house.

After his mother's death in 1887, Antony brought in the architect Henry Woodyer – one of Butterfield's few pupils – to make substantial alterations, including the extension of the dining room and remodelling of the staircase hall. In the twentieth century structural problems meant that both the clock tower and conservatory had to be demolished, but perhaps because of its very size and elaboration, Tyntesfield escaped any major internal erosion of its Victorian character. Its future looked bleak in 2001, following the death of Antony Gibbs's reclusive bachelor grandson, as he bequeathed the house and estate to all his father's descendants jointly, forcing a sale of the estate, house and its contents. Fortunately, the National Trust stepped in, and with the aid of a large grant from the National Heritage Memorial Fund and a very successful public appeal, was able to purchase Tyntesfield for preservation intact.

Right: *The chapel, designed by Arthur Blomfield and built in 1873–75. Its stained glass is by James Powell of Whitefriars, London.*

Below: *The library, which was completely remodelled by John Norton in 1863–65 with a high arch-braced timber roof, oak panelling and a marble Gothic fireplace.*

G.F. WATTS R.A.
LONDON

1870

CHRISTIAN DUTY

Country-house ownership offered pleasure and status, but for the Victorians it also embodied responsibilities. The sense of social duty which had been encouraged by religious revivals earlier in the century – first Evangelical and then Tractarian – was bolstered in the 1870s by the reformist zeal of Gladstone's first government, from 1868 to 1874. The Liberal programme of reforms – from the creation of school boards to the disestablishment of the Church of Ireland – was supported by the Whig nobility and in particular the Marquess of Westminster, whose loyalty was repaid in Gladstone's dissolution honours when he was elevated to a dukedom. The new duke's belief that the landed classes had a duty to improve the welfare of the rest of the population was symbolized by the way that he opened his park, gardens and art collections to the public.

Although Eaton was in essence a modern house, public curiosity about the greatest aristocratic dynasty of the north west, and the estate's closeness to Chester and Liverpool, made it a major tourist attraction. Yet the seriousness of purpose so evident on the Duke of Westminster's domain was echoed even in houses that were far less well known. At Longleat, which although open to the public bore no resemblance to the enormous attraction that it became after the Second World War, the Marquess of Bath's redecoration of its interiors was designed in large part to accommodate his new collection of Italian Old Master paintings, a subject on which he possessed considerable scholarly knowledge. Cragside, although originally acquired for its sporting amenities, allowed Lord Armstrong to demonstrate how the discoveries that he had made about hydraulic and hydro-electric power could serve domestic purposes; the house had not only an art collection and a museum, but also an observatory and a laboratory.

The high seriousness of the 1870s – soon to seem an almost admonitory contrast with the hedonism of the Edwardian era – was most evident in the religious life of these houses. Country-house owners had usually built private chapels because their parish church was too remote, or because they lacked sympathy with local churchmanship, or, as with Roman Catholics, were Non-Conformist. The architecturally undemonstrative tradition of private Catholic worship changed in the mid-nineteenth century: Carlton Towers was not unusual in the way that a house with a long and discreet tradition of recusancy was transformed into a proud statement of a family's religious identity. This was a result of the relaxation in attitudes to non-Anglican forms of religious expression that lay behind many of Gladstone's legislative reforms. But for the Duke of Westminster, well provided with estate churches, the building of Alfred Waterhouse's great chapel at Eaton – the setting for prayers for the entire household at nine every morning and for choral evensong every Sunday – simply proclaimed the unquestioning piety that lay at the heart of all that he hoped to achieve.

The chapel and clock tower at Eaton Hall, Cheshire. In the foreground is G. F. Watts's statue of the Duke of Westminster's ancestor Hugh Lupus, Earl of Chester, completed in 1879.

CARLTON TOWERS, YORKSHIRE

From the top of the clock tower that soars above Carlton Towers there is a panoramic view across the flat landscape south of Selby to the massive power stations at Drax, Eggborough and Ferry Bridge, looming on the horizon. The house's blunt Gothic silhouette is unexpected enough in this industrial setting; it is perhaps even more surprising that this great Victorian mansion survives in immaculate order, the centre of a flourishing estate.

Carlton Towers is no less extraordinary when seen close up, rich in heraldic ornament that proclaims the ancestry of the Stapleton family, who by the mid-nineteenth century had been seated here for over five hundred years. Carlton's Victorian splendour is in fact only skin-deep. The medieval house was rebuilt as a compact three-storey block in 1614, to which a long, thin east wing was added in 1777 to house a chapel and stables. The chapel was essential, as the Stapletons had – to their considerable financial and social cost – stayed loyal to the old faith after the Reformation. In 1795 Thomas Stapleton laid claim to the dormant barony of Beaumont, a case that was finally resolved in 1840, when his great-nephew was called to the House of Lords as 8th Baron Beaumont. He marked his ennoblement by remodelling Carlton in a subdued Gothic fashion, but this celebration of his lineage was accompanied by a severing of family tradition: he joined the Church of England and converted the chapel and stables at Carlton into reception rooms.

When he died in 1854 his heir was only six months old. The new Lord Beaumont came of age at a moment when the Roman Catholic Church was undergoing a great revival in England. Among his contemporaries at Oxford was the 3rd Marquess of Bute, and Lord Beaumont, like him, converted to Roman Catholicism. It is possible that his architectural ambitions were encouraged by Lord Bute's new buildings at Cardiff Castle and elsewhere, but his financial resources were no match for his friend's. Nonetheless, he set to work at once,

Above: *Carlton Towers from the south, photographed in 1994.*

Right: *The outer hall. The room is largely E. W. Pugin's creation but was fitted out by J. F. Bentley, who designed the stained glass, the tiled floor and the metal table with a green marble top. The bust, by Patrick MacDowell, is a portrait of the 8th Lord Beaumont.*

and in 1873 commissioned A. W. N. Pugin's eldest son, Edward Welby Pugin, to draw up a scheme for rebuilding and enlarging Carlton Towers. In 1875 Pugin published a design which envisaged doubling the house in size by attaching a vast staircase tower to the east end of the east range, which would lead to a new chapel and 'baron's hall', both on an epic scale.

Lord Beaumont could never have afforded it. Pugin was an architect whose ambition often outsoared his means. He was touchy, even a little paranoid, with a well-deserved reputation for public disputes. Yet, as his work at Scarisbrick Hall shows, he was an accomplished designer who successfully developed his father's style into the heavier and more eclectic idiom that became fashionable in the 1850s, and his friendship with Lady Scarisbrick reveals that he could have happy relationships with his clients. He cannot take full responsibility for the Carlton scheme, for Lord Beaumont's romantic temperament was quite capable of losing touch with reality all by itself. When work at Carlton began he was away in Spain, fighting for the pretender to its throne.

Pugin refaced the house in buff-coloured cement grooved to look like stone, heightened the Jacobean staircase tower and added another tower to contain a new front staircase. He replaced a large, plain clock tower, added by Lord Beaumont's father, with one far higher and more flamboyant in outline, capped with four carved figures of talbots, the supporters of the Beaumont arms. The final touch to this bristling skyline was the turrets in which Pugin hid the chimneystacks.

Barely two years after work had begun, Lord Beaumont quarrelled with his architect, and the interiors of Carlton Towers were completed by John Francis Bentley, like Pugin a Roman Catholic, but otherwise different from him in almost every way. Bentley – who later turned down a commission from Lord Beaumont to design a block of flats in Knightsbridge on the grounds that it was an unwise

Above: *The Card Room. Its linenfold panelling was carved by J. Erskine Knox. The silvered chandelier is a variation on a design used by Bentley throughout his new rooms.*

Left: *The Venetian Drawing Room, decorated by Bentley, who designed the chimneypiece, chairs and curtains. The fireplace tiles are by William de Morgan.*

speculation for his client – was not a designer likely to tempt a patron into extravagance. His interiors at Carlton are notable for disciplined luxuriousness: expense is not spared, but neither is it wasted.

Bentley is usually associated with the Byzantine splendours of his masterpiece, Westminster Cathedral, commissioned in 1895, but he was in essence a Gothic designer. He was one of the generation that, in the mid-1860s, turned against the assertiveness and eclecticism of the High Victorian style practised by such architects as Butterfield and Burges. Bentley's Gothic buildings are notable for austerity of outline as well as delicacy of detail. He might, therefore, have seemed an unlikely choice to complete Carlton Towers, yet when occasion demanded he could rise to E. W. Pugin's challenge, most notably in the mighty heraldic fireplace in the principal reception room, the Venetian Drawing Room. Bentley had been trained in the office of Henry Clutton, who was then in partnership with Lord Bute's architect at Cardiff, William Burges. According to Bentley's daughter, Winefride de l'Hôpital, Burges 'encouraged the love of rich and glowing colour so strongly emphasized in Bentley's earliest designs and probably impressed him with the attention he bestowed on figure drawing in decorative sculpture.'

Like Burges, Bentley preferred to work with a small circle of trusted craftsmen. At Carlton he employed Nathaniel Westlake and his firm, Lavers, Barraud & Westlake, for figure painting and stained glass. The splendid woodcarving is by J. Erskine Knox, metalwork is by Longden & Co., and William de Morgan supplied tiles. Bentley designed every detail, including the tiled floor in the outer hall and the green and terracotta silk velvets used for upholstery and curtains. Most of his work is concentrated in the three reception rooms that occupy the east wing: the Venetian Drawing Room, Card Room and Gallery. The drawing room is one of the finest and best preserved of all Victorian country-house reception rooms. It takes its name from a set of Venetian glass that Bentley had discovered in storage; the black-panelled dado incorporates showcases for its display. The walls, which at first glance seem to be covered in golden stamped leather, are in fact faced with plaster moulded into a pomegranate pattern. The cornice is decorated with 'B's', for Beaumont, alternating with heraldic roses, lions and shells.

Careful although Bentley may have been in his expenditure, Lord Beaumont was not, and when he died in 1892 he left debts of nearly a quarter-million pounds. Fortunately his brother, who succeeded him, had married an heiress. Their daughter, Mona, who became Baroness Beaumont in her own right when her father was killed in a shooting accident in 1895, married Lord Howard of Glossop, heir presumptive to the dukedom of Norfolk. Their son Miles, who was brought up at Carlton, duly succeeded as 17th Duke of Norfolk in 1975, uniting the Stapleton estates with those of the Fitzalan-Howards and ensuring the unbroken line of hereditary succession at Carlton that goes back to the Norman Conquest.

The view from the top of Carlton's clock tower.

CRAGSIDE, NORTHUMBERLAND

Crowning the precipitous heights of a ravine carved by the Debdon Burn, Cragside was described by one contemporary as 'the palace of a modern magician'. When its gabled west tower catches the setting sun, it does indeed suggest the Victorian Valhalla of a plutocratic Wotan. Moreover, the career of its creator, William Armstrong, suggests an affinity with Wagner's power-hungry god of the battle-field. He revolutionized the armaments industry by inventing the Armstrong gun, which fired a shell rather than a ball and was made of steel instead of iron. By 1900, when Lord Armstrong died at the age of ninety, having been ennobled thirteen years before, his factory at Elswick, just outside Newcastle – over which he had presided with a patriarchal disdain for organized labour – was rivalled as a manufacturer of armaments and battleships only by Krupps of Germany.

Above: *The entrance front, mostly built in 1872–74. On the right is the drawing-room wing, added in 1883–84.*

Left: *Cragside looming above a steel footbridge over the Debdon Burn. The bridge, erected in the early 1870s, was probably made at William Armstrong's factory at Elswick.*

Yet in personal terms, Lord Armstrong was the antithesis of all that this implies. Mild-mannered, kindly and philanthropic, he was absorbed throughout his life by the intellectual challenges of scientific experiment. A loving husband, keen fisherman and collector of modern art, he celebrated his happy domestic life at Cragside with an inscription on the chimneypiece in the dining-room inglenook, 'East or West Hame's Best'. It was his good fortune to choose an architect with the skill and temperament to create a house that is as compellingly sublime outside as it is comfortably domestic within.

In 1869 Armstrong bought a picture by the painter J. C. Horsley that was so big that he decided to extend the gallery-cum-banqueting hall in his house at Jesmond on the outskirts of Newcastle. It was almost certainly Horsley who recommended Armstrong to employ Richard Norman Shaw for the task, since five years earlier Shaw had designed a house for him, at Willesley in Kent. This was among the earliest buildings to exemplify Shaw's 'Old English' style, the first wholly convincing domestic alternative to modern Gothic or historical revivalism. 'Old English' is a picturesque blend of vernacular motifs –

half-timbering, tile-hanging – forged into the bold forms that Shaw had learned from the Gothic Revival, and in particular two of the architects under whom he had trained, Anthony Salvin and George Edmund Street. Moreover, Shaw had begun his career as a pupil of William Burn, and his great success as a country-house designer was based in part on a Burn-like grasp of the importance of good planning and services.

Armstrong was in his sixties by the time that Shaw first visited Cragside, and he seems to have planned the house as a retirement project. It was to occupy him for over twenty-five years in a long sequence of piecemeal additions and alterations: it is a testament to Shaw's skill that although the finished house is as complex in its composition as in its building history, in most views it composes with memorable force. Armstrong bought the site, near Rothbury, in 1863. He built a small house for shooting and fishing parties and landscaped the grounds, which he steadily enlarged to 1,729 acres, laid out with 31 miles of carriage drives winding through seven million newly planted trees and shrubs. Shaw recalled that he sketched his design for rebuilding Cragside – his first large country house – one afternoon in 1869 while his host was out shooting. However, initially he seems to have been asked simply to add a new wing on the north side, with a library, dining room and additional bedrooms, on which work began in 1870.

When Shaw first saw Cragside he wrote that the estate had 'wonderful hydraulic machines that do all sorts of things'. Partly to avoid water shortages, Armstrong had created a large lake on the Debdon. It was dammed for a hydraulic ram that not only supplied the house's water but also powered revolving stands for plant pots in the conservatories. The water supply was so copious that Shaw was able to incorporate a big tile-lined plunge pool into his new wing, as part of a Turkish-bath suite. In the 1870s Armstrong made another

Above: *The library, the house's main living room, completed in 1874. In the corner is the globe of a gas light converted to take electricity in 1880. The other electrical fittings were added in 1895 to replace the original bare bulbs.*

Right (above): *The picture gallery, originally a museum for Armstrong's natural-history specimens. Shaw left the iron stanchions supporting the roof exposed; they were boxed in much later.* (below): *The dining room. Its fireplace, which encloses an inglenook, is based on a medieval arch in the kitchen at Fountains Abbey, Yorkshire.*

lake higher up the stream, which was also dammed. This was linked to a turbine which supplied electricity for the house, an extraordinarily pioneering move: in 1878 Armstrong installed an arc-lamp to illuminate his picture gallery and in 1880 Cragside became the first house in the world to be lit by the incandescent carbon-filament bulbs invented by Joseph Swan of Newcastle, a friend of Armstrong.

Yet Armstrong was not interested solely in technology: he appreciated his new lighting for its artistic impact, writing in 1881 that 'the lamps are for the most part used without glass shades and present a very beautiful and star-like appearance.' They illuminated some of Shaw's most attractive Aesthetic Movement rooms, which weave Oriental and Arts and Crafts inspiration into his 'Old English' idiom. In the library, designed as a setting for pictures and Japanese blue-and-white ceramics as much as books, stained glass was provided by Morris & Co., and the light oak dado was embellished with foliage delicately carved by James Forsyth. Shaw himself designed the room's suite of light, ebonized chairs, their backs upholstered in leather stamped with a pomegranate pattern.

In 1872, Shaw exhibited at the Royal Academy a design for remodelling the south and west fronts, and for heightening the house's modest tower. Armstrong accepted this in a revised form which included a long eastern extension to contain a museum for his geological and ornithological specimens, terminating in a high tower used by him initially as an observatory. Then, in the early 1880s, he decided to sell his estate at Jesmond to the City of Newcastle and make Cragside his principal home. Shaw returned to add the drawing-room wing, attached to the end of the museum, which was converted into a top-lit picture gallery. Completed in 1884, the drawing room magnificently demonstrates the turn in Shaw's domestic designs away from 'Old English' to Renaissance forms. It formed a suitable backdrop for the grand entertaining that Armstrong undertook in his later years: the King of Siam and Shah of Persia visited Cragside in 1889 and the Crown Prince of Afghanistan in 1895 – all came seeking to purchase armaments from the Elswick factories.

Armstrong and his wife had no children, and on his death in 1900 his estates – which included Bamburgh Castle on the Northumberland coast – were inherited by his great-nephew, who became the 1st Lord Armstrong of the 2nd creation. His unwise business investments prompted the sale of most of Cragside's art collection in 1910. Following the death of his son in 1972, the house and its estate were accepted by the nation in lieu of death duties and given to the National Trust.

The drawing room, Shaw's final addition to Cragside. The magnificent chimneypiece, decorated in an Elizabethan manner, was designed by one of his most gifted assistants, W. R. Lethaby and carved by Farmer and Brindley.

EATON HALL, CHESHIRE

In 1872 Charles Locke Eastlake published *A History of the Gothic Revival*, the first book-length account of its subject and still an invaluable source for the study of Victorian Gothic. He devotes a lengthy description and a full-page plate to Eaton Hall, the Cheshire seat of the Marquess of Westminster. Originally a seventeenth-century house, it had been rebuilt in a flamboyant Gothic manner to the designs of William Porden in 1804–12 and extended in a style to match in 1823–25. Eastlake's judgment was cool: 'The size of the building alone would make it imposing, but the distribution of the parts, as in many efforts of that day, is more suited to the outline of an Italian composition than that of a Gothic design, while the character of the details is of a pseudo-ecclesiastical kind ... the noble mansions of old England had still to be studied.'

However, as Eastlake added in a footnote: 'Since this description was written, Mr. A. Waterhouse has been employed by the present Marquis of Westminster to remodel the building, which will thus undergo considerable alteration and improvement. The internal decorations will be of an exceedingly rich and beautiful description.' Despite alterations and extensions by William Burn in 1846–51, Porden's house failed to satisfy mid-Victorian ideas of architectural propriety: its window tracery was cast iron and its Gothic vaults were plaster. The effect of the interiors depended to a great degree on upholstery and wall-hangings, which after sixty years had lost their Regency sparkle.

In 1869 Hugh Lupus Grosvenor succeeded his father as 3rd Marquess; five years later he was created 1st Duke of Westminster. Although the Grosvenors had been seated at Eaton, a few miles south of Chester, since the fifteenth century, it was the development in the early nineteenth century of the family's estates in Mayfair and Belgravia that propelled them to the top league of the aristocracy. When he inherited, the Duke's annual income from his London estate was £115,000; by the end of the century it had risen to £250,000. In addition, since his agricultural estates were largely devoted to dairy

Above: *The garden front, which faced east, photographed in 1901.*

Left: *A detail of the south wing of Eaton Hall. The library occupied the ground floor.*

farming, he suffered far less than landowners in the south or east from the collapse of cereal prices in the late 1870s.

The Duke had a deep sense of the responsibilities of his station. On his death in 1900, *The Times* recalled him as 'a fine example of the great noble who, while following the same pursuits and amusements as other Englishmen of wealth and leisure, devotes a great part of his time to the service of those less fortunate than himself ... he could pass from the race courses to a missionary meeting without incurring the censure of even the strictest.' He gave with unstinting generosity to charity; the house and park at Eaton were open to the public; and he undertook the rebuilding of estate buildings on a heroic scale. The historian Edward Hubbard has calculated that the Duke paid for four churches and chapels; eight parsonages and large houses for key estate staff; some 15 schools; five farms; 300 hundred cottages, lodges and smithies; two factories; two inns; and about 12 other buildings.

The very unexpectedness of the Duke's choice of architect for a new Eaton Hall – it was Waterhouse's first large country house – is an indication of his thoughtful approach to architectural patronage and design. These were matters that he never delegated. For example, most of the new estate buildings were designed in a picturesque Cheshire vernacular by the Chester-based John Douglas, with whom the Duke had a happy and trusting relationship extending over thirty years. As Douglas's drawings reveal, his patron took a close interest in the detail of every last cottage, pencilling in both practical and aesthetic amendments.

It seems likely that the Duke was influenced by the acclaim given to Waterhouse following his success in the competition for Manchester Town Hall in 1867, a triumph that had depended in great part on the ingenious planning of the winning scheme. Eaton was in some ways an even more challenging project, as Waterhouse was required to preserve as far as possible the structure of Porden's Eaton; in addition, the house was built and altered in phases over a period of almost thirty years, providing plenty of opportunity for the Duke to change his mind as work progressed. By May 1870 the builder, George Smith – who had also been employed for the restoration of Alnwick – had begun work; the initial contract price was £580,000.

As well as requiring a complete recasting of the existing house, which included raising it by an extra floor for new bedrooms, the Duke asked Waterhouse to add a staircase and library wing at the south end of the house, a wing to accommodate bachelor bedrooms at its north-west corner, a new kitchen wing on the north and a family wing on the north-east corner, which was designed almost as a separate house. This family and service accommodation was extended to the east with a great apsed chapel.

As at Manchester Town Hall, Waterhouse worked in a free form of Gothic heavily influenced by France, his own, very individual version of the High Victorian style. Even by the early 1870s, it was unfashion-

The entrance hall in 1932. The tapestries are part of the celebrated Holy Grail *set designed by Edward Burne-Jones and woven by Morris & Co. in 1890–94 for Stanmore Hall in Middlesex. They were acquired by the 2nd Duke of Westminster in 1920.*

HONI SOIT QUI

able, but it is hard to conceive of Eaton being designed in any other way: its enormous bulk would have looked ridiculous dressed up as an 'Old English' mansion. Waterhouse did all in his power to give its exterior the Gothic vitality that Porden's had lacked, with high-pitched roofs, pedimented dormers and spired turrets, glittering with iron crestings and tiles arranged in colourful patterns. The Duke rejected his suggestion for a tower over the library wing, but did not object to the enormous height – 185 feet – of the chapel's clock tower.

The quality of the architectural carving and decorative painting in the interior was magnificent. Most of the principal living rooms were simply redecorated, but the library, 30 feet by 90 feet, was entirely new, Gothic in feel but eclectically modern in detail, with walnut fireplaces inlaid with boxwood and mother of pearl, painted decoration by Heaton, Butler & Bayne and tapestries designed by Gertrude Jekyll. This attention to aesthetic detail was matched by technological excellence. From the start, Eaton had gas for cooking and lighting – its gas house was also designed by Waterhouse – and it was converted to electricity for lighting in 1887.

The house's large stable court is an intriguing blend of Waterhousian Gothic with the relaxed vernacular that John Douglas had used so attractively in the estate buildings. Was this a deliberate move away from what must have seemed at times the almost oppressive magnificence of the new Eaton Hall? The 1st Duke's successor, his playboy grandson Bendor, revived social life at Eaton on a grand scale after the First World War, and the 2nd Duke made efforts to adapt the house to modern tastes by adding fitted bathrooms, whitewashing some of the painted decoration and thinning out the furniture, with effects recorded in *Country Life*'s 1932 photographs of the interiors. After the Second World War, the house was let to the army for use as an officers' training college, but with the end of military conscription in 1960 the War Office surrendered the lease. The present Duke was then only a schoolboy, and assuming that no duke of Westminster would ever again want to live at Eaton Hall, his trustees had it demolished, sparing little more than the stables and chapel. After the 6th Duke came of age in 1967 he built a much smaller house on the site of the old.

Above: *The library. This was the major new interior designed by Alfred Waterhouse.*

Left: *The main staircase, lined with suits of armour once at Strawberry Hill, Horace Walpole's Gothic villa in Twickenham.*

In his celebrated book on British domestic architecture, *Das Englische Haus* (1904–05), the German critic Hermann Muthesius lavished praise on the estate buildings designed by John Douglas for the 1st Duke of Westminster: 'their fresh and natural character shows them up to great advantage against Alfred Waterhouse's main house'. Douglas's work for the Duke encompasses lodges, substantial houses for estate staff and a great variety of cottages, all of which use decorative brickwork, half-timbering and other vernacular motifs with memorably picturesque effect. However, for certain important landmarks, notably Eccleston Hill Lodge, Douglas revealed that he was capable of a flamboyant Gothic that was a match for Waterhouse.

EATON ESTATE BUILDINGS This page (top left): *The Upper Belgrave Lodge at Eaton, 1877*; (top right): *The Stud Lodge at Eaton, 1881–82*; (bottom left): *The Paddocks, Eccleston, built in 1882–83 for the Hon. Cecil Parker, the 1st Duke's agent*; (bottom right): *A pair of cottages at Eccleston, 1882*.

Right: *Eccleston Hill Lodge, 1881*.

LONGLEAT HOUSE, WILTSHIRE

Longleat's fame as a prodigy house of Elizabethan England has obscured its Victorian significance. The great hall apart, its principal interiors retain very few traces of Sir John Thynne, who bought the dissolved Carthusian priory in 1541, and over the next thirty-five years converted its remains into the most coherent and refined Classical mansion of its time. Instead, Longleat's state apartments are one of the most spectacular achievements of nineteenth-century interior design, a sumptuous and perfectly preserved monument to the taste, wealth and confidence of the Victorian aristocracy at its zenith.

When he came of age in 1852, John Alexander Thynne, 3rd Marquess of Bath, entered into a golden inheritance. His father had died in 1837 and during Lord Bath's fifteen-year minority his mother had cared for his estates so well that she was able to hand them over debt free, with £50,000 in the bank. Moreover, Longleat itself was in good order. It had been restored for the 1st Marquess of Bath at enormous expense in two phases between 1806 and 1830 by the architect Sir Jeffry Wyatville, resulting in a house that was widely praised for its comfort and convenience. The new Lord Bath therefore turned his attention to agricultural improvements. By 1883 his rental income was £46,000 a year.

Lord Bath followed a long-standing aristocratic tradition by departing on a Grand Tour of the Continent when he turned twenty-one. Unlike many of his predecessors on the journey, however, he had a genuine love of art and architecture and was overwhelmed by Italy, to which he remained deeply attached for the rest of his life. In 1867 the government appointed him 'ambassador extraordinary' to Venice, and it was probably while he was there that he began to collect Italian

Above: *The south front of Longleat House.*

Left: *The saloon, decorated in 1874. This was the first of the interiors undertaken by J. D. Crace for the 3rd Marquess of Bath.*

pictures, thus beginning the process that would lead, in 1874, to his decision to redecorate Longleat. By then Wyatville's interiors doubtless seemed tired and old-fashioned: his principal remaining reception room at Longleat, the Green Library, reveals that he had in essence provided modern, Neo-Classical rooms touched up with a little strapwork and with simple plaster ceilings in Elizabethan style. To Victorian eyes his work must have lacked colour and heft. Over the next six years the house was transformed with results that recall the Italianate interiors at Alnwick Castle, created twenty years before. But whereas the Duke of Northumberland had gone to Italy to find designers and craftsmen capable of executing such schemes, Lord Bath needed to look no further than Wigmore Street in London.

The designer he chose was John Dibblee Crace, head of the fifth generation of the Crace firm of interior decorators. The Craces had by then been working at the top level of British society for over eighty years, supplying, for example, furniture and interiors for the Prince Regent at Carlton House and Brighton Pavilion and for Queen Victoria and Prince Albert at Windsor Castle. J. D. Crace's father, John Gregory Crace, had formed a close working relationship with A.W. N. Pugin, which found its finest expression in the interiors of the Palace of Westminster. After Pugin's death in 1852 he continued to supply textiles, wallpapers and furniture made to Pugin's designs or in a version of his manner.

Yet J. G. Crace had always been prepared to work in a Classical manner when required, and at the 1862 International Exhibition in London he and his son showed furniture and decorative schemes designed in a Renaissance manner, in part inspired by a tour of Italy made by J. D. Crace in 1859. He returned there in 1863 with Charles Barry Jr for an intensive study of Renaissance interiors, especially in Mantua and Venice. It was here that he developed his deep interest in the use of colour to enhance architectural structure, and many of the buildings that he recorded in detail in his sketchbooks were to form models for his work at Longleat.

Lord Bath's new interiors had got off to an abortive start in 1873 when he commissioned the architect George Fox to design a new ceiling for the saloon, formerly the long gallery. The dull result was brought to life by Crace's painted scheme, in which deep blue, green and red grounds are embellished with white arabesque ornament. This imitated the way that Renaissance decorators used small-scale ornament on strongly coloured backgrounds, as Crace had observed in the Palazzo del Tè, Mantua. The room is hung with tapestries collected by Lord Bath against a backdrop of 245 yards of Utrecht velvet, supplied by Crace, who also designed the saloon's alabaster doorcases and olive-green and maroon silk curtains. The towering white marble chimneypiece, carved by George Sinclair, a London-based architectural sculptor, incorporates two muscular male figures copied from a chimneypiece in the Doge's Palace in Venice.

The State Drawing Room, where Crace created a fusion of genuine Italian Renaissance elements, seventeenth-century textiles and modern ceiling paintings copied from Veronese, as a setting for Lord Bath's Old Master paintings.

The other rooms similarly fuse decorative painting of high quality with new architectural fittings designed and supplied by Crace and antique elements collected by Lord Bath. As their correspondence in the archives at Longleat show, they jointly undertook research on suitable Italian models for the schemes. In 1874, for example, Lord Bath sent Crace a volume of Francesco Zanotto's 1858 book on the Doge's Palace, drawing his attention to an illustration that might serve as model for the ceiling in the State Drawing Room, writing, 'If one can only find a drawing at all suitable one cannot do better than follow it closely. I am fully convinced that for two hundred and seventy years there has been nothing original that has been really good except perhaps some of the Adams & such like works.'

The State Drawing Room, designed as a setting for Lord Bath's finest Italian Old Master paintings, was the most expensive of Crace's new interiors – he charged £1,132 for it in 1877. The ceiling was once again by George Fox, whose suggestion of decorating it with *putti* was adopted, but with Crace's carefully considered colours. This scheme is the setting for copies of ceiling paintings by Veronese and Zelotti in the Library of St Mark's, Venice, commissioned by Lord Bath in Italy in 1875; the ceiling painting in the bay, however, is an Italian work of the sixteenth or seventeenth centuries, and the frieze is attributed to the seventeenth-century painter Piero Liberi. Lord Bath's pictures are hung against a red Genoa velvet, which came from an Italian church and was believed by Crace to be seventeenth-century.

Intriguing elements of Islamic design are incorporated into this ensemble, perhaps reflecting Crace's sensitivity to the Islamic influence on Venetian architecture and design: his grey marble door-cases are Renaissance in style, but they incorporate white marble mouldings inlaid with coloured marbles in a manner that Crace compared to 'the Taj at Agra'. Here, as elsewhere in the house, the door furniture is made of damascened steel, in origin an Islamic technique, and Crace had Wilton weave the carpet (originally red, but later dyed green) after a Persian original in the South Kensington – now the Victoria and Albert – Museum.

Crace's work at Longleat was finished in 1882, having cost some £8,000. His pride in what he had achieved is apparent in his description of the work in his book *The Art of Colour Decoration*, published in 1912. A record of his beliefs in the value of polychromatic decoration in architecture, it was by then deeply old-fashioned; Crace had closed his firm and retired in 1899. Lord Bath had died in 1896, having lived long enough to see the impact of the agricultural recession, and although his estates fared better than many, his last years were clouded by depression exacerbated by doubts about the future. It may have seemed an omen that he died not at Longleat but in a hotel overlooking the Grand Canal in his beloved Venice. Nevertheless, Longleat not only survived the twentieth century, it flourished; it remains the home of the Thynnes as well as one of England's most popular tourist attractions.

The Lower Dining Room. Its plaster ceiling was designed by Crace and executed by George Jackson & Sons of London.

1880

FROM IDYLL TO ELEGY

By the end of the 1870s Britain's agricultural prosperity had come to an abrupt end. A series of bad harvests was accompanied by improvements in transatlantic shipping which led to the market being flooded with cheap grain from the newly opened American prairies. In 1868 Britain had produced almost eighty per cent of the food it consumed; by the end of the century most was imported. The illusion that country houses were the embodiment of agricultural wealth could no longer be sustained, especially in the grain-producing counties of the south and east. By the mid-1880s the association of country houses with political power was also fraying: following franchise reform in 1884, landowners were for the first time ever in a minority in the House of Commons.

Yet country houses continued to be built. Occasionally this was because, as at Stokesay Court and Waddesdon Manor, they were the culmination of a process of estate acquisition that had begun in the 1870s. Ferdinand Rothschild recognized that the timing of his purchase of Waddesdon had not been good, as land prices fell in the 1880s, but he never considered the estate as an investment – by the end of the century he drew an income from Waddesdon of £6,000 a year, exactly the amount it had produced in 1874, despite the fact that in the intervening time he had spent over £1 million in building the house and improving the estate. The Rothschild wealth could take that in its stride, but when John Derby Allcroft died in 1893 did he sense that economic reality had dimmed his dream of setting up his eldest son at Stokesay Court as a landed gentleman?

1890

Other patrons of new houses, such as Lord Coleridge at Chanter's House, were rich enough to build on a scale to match their rank, but – unlike so many of his predecessors as Lord Chief Justice – he showed no inclination to acquire more than a few acres to accompany his house. Some aristocrats could draw on industrial or commercial revenues to rebuild houses on traditional estates, although few were so ambitious as Lord Windsor, who paid for the extremely costly Hewell Grange with his income from Cardiff ground rents. For him, the new house was justified as a setting for his art collection and for entertaining on a grand scale, but even while his family still lived there its aesthetic atmosphere acquired an elegiac tinge: as Lady Windsor reflected in 1932, nine years after her husband's death, 'Had we had any idea how quickly the circumstances of life in this country, and indeed throughout the world, would change, I do not think we should have dreamt of building a house of that scale.'

The garden lobby and a corner of the hall at Hewell Grange, Worcestershire, photographed in 1902.

THE CHANTER'S HOUSE, DEVON

Coleridges have always lived in Devon, but they came to Ottery St Mary only in 1760, when John Coleridge was appointed headmaster of the King's School. Here he raised four daughters and seven sons, the youngest of whom, born in 1772, was Samuel Taylor Coleridge. He never forgot the landscape of his childhood: the little town clustering around St Mary's church on the Cornhill, overlooking the broad valley of the River Otter, was poignantly recalled in his poem 'Frost at Midnight'.

The second eldest son, James, was very different from his maverick genius of a brother. A hard-headed career soldier, he married a local heiress and in 1796 bought one of the town's principal houses. Until 1900 it was known as 'Heath's Court', after its eighteenth-century owners, but it was conveyed to the Colonel – as he was always known – under its original name, the Chanter's House. The most substantial of the buildings that are grouped, almost like a cathedral close, around the great fourteenth-century church, it has medieval origins, but was in essence a seventeenth-century house disguised behind a plain Georgian façade.

In 1838 the house was inherited by the Colonel's second son, Sir John Coleridge, who had been made a judge three years earlier. At Oxford he had formed a lasting friendship with John Keble, whose biography he wrote. His High Church beliefs were shared by his eldest son, John Duke Coleridge, also a lawyer, who went up to Balliol in 1839, at the stormy height of the Oxford Movement. There he was spellbound by John Newman, who became a lifelong

Above: *The Chanter's House from the west. The large wing on the left houses the vast library. The tower of the parish church is visible in the centre; on the right is a dovecote by the Devon-born Arts and Crafts designer Walter Cave, built in 1896.*

Right: *The garden front. Butterfield encased but did not hide the Georgian façade of the existing house.*

influence. Father and son had similar artistic and literary interests and together they extended Heath's Court with a modest one-storey drawing room, landscaped its original 30-acre grounds, and paid for the restoration of the parish church. This brought the architect William Butterfield into their circle, the result of an introduction by Sir John's brother, Edward. He had been a driving force behind the foundation in 1844 of a training college for missionaries, St Augustine's, Canterbury, the architect's first major commission.

In a lecture on the restoration of the church published in 1851, John Duke Coleridge praised Butterfield's 'great skill and abilities ... and the masculine severity of his taste.' Despite the architect's reputation for chilly puritanism, the Coleridges enjoyed his company; he asked their advice on personal and professional matters, and sought their support when his designs were interfered with by unfeeling patrons. Many stories about Butterfield passed into family legend: when a visitor complained to him about the punishing discomfort of his new pews in St Mary's, he replied, 'But are you not a little undersized?'

REYNELL

In 1880 John Duke Coleridge's brilliant legal career was crowned by his appointment as Lord Chief Justice. His new rank turned his thoughts to rebuilding his family home as a country seat that would also be in part a memorial to his wife, who had died suddenly in 1878. This was Butterfield's second, and last, substantial country-house commission, after Milton Ernest Hall, some twenty-five years before. A hall was added on the east, so that the former entrance became the garden front. Although Butterfield raised the Georgian façade by an extra half-timbered storey, with three high dormers (later hung with shingles), and encased it in brick, the old house remains visible, like a fossil in a High Victorian cliff face. This may reflect a wish by Lord Coleridge to preserve its memory, but characteristically Butterfield stressed rather than smoothed over the resulting jerkiness by boldly emphasizing the cornice line of the Georgian house and securing deep changes of level, down to the one-storey drawing room and back up to his new, monumental library wing on the west.

The visitor enters a small, low porch, and then turns at right angles into a tall, brightly lit outer hall. Another right-angle turn leads into the dark inner hall. Straight ahead is the door to the house's finest interior, the vast library, designed to house Lord Coleridge's 18,000 books. It was richly furnished with busts of heroes and friends, including Newman and Matthew Arnold, plaster casts of Classical statues, fragments of medieval sculpture and fireplaces with marble reliefs by Lord Coleridge's favourite sculptor, Frederick Thrupp.

The Chanter's House embodied a pious, scholarly strand in mid-Victorian culture that already seemed over solemn by the time it was completed. Yet it suited the Coleridges perfectly, and was preserved by them with atmospheric intactness until 2006, when the house was sold and its contents dispersed at auction.

Above: *A plaster cast of the tomb effigy of Lady Coleridge, carved by Frederick Thrupp, in a room opening off the library gallery.*

Left: *The library. The large drawings after Michelangelo are by Lady Coleridge.*

HEWELL GRANGE, WORCESTERSHIRE

In the mid-1880s, a circle of friends who had coalesced around two leading Conservative politicians, Lord Curzon and Arthur Balfour, began to attract attention for their intriguing mixture of *joie de vivre* and high-mindedness. Their interest in art, literature, languages and philosophy was thought so unusual that they were nicknamed 'the Souls'. Almost all this group of families loosely linked by marriage and love affairs – the Wyndhams, Charterises, Tennants, Custs, Windsors and Grenfells – collected modern paintings and sculpture and took great pleasure in creating harmonious interiors. They were also responsible for two of the great houses of the 1880s, Clouds in Wiltshire, commissioned from Philip Webb by Percy and Madeline Wyndham, and Hewell Grange, just outside Redditch, designed by Thomas Garner for Viscount and Viscountess Windsor.

Above: *Hewell Grange photographed in 1993, across the remains of its herbaceous parterre garden, laid out in the early 1890s by the head gardener, Andrew Pettigrew.*

Left: *Lord and Lady Windsor with their son and daughter in the hall at Hewell Grange, painted in 1908 by William Nicholson (Private Collection).*

Contemporaries delighted in the contrast between the two houses: in 1895, Lady Windsor's mother wrote from Hewell that 'I returned from white and blue Clouds, charming in its way, to this house blazing with gorgeous Italian colour.'

Shortly after he came of age in 1878, Lord Windsor asked the architect G. F. Bodley to inspect the eighteenth-century house at Hewell. Bodley produced plans for enlarging it, but it soon became clear that the necessary alterations would amount virtually to a rebuilding, and so it was decided to build a new house on a site some distance from the old, on the edge of an existing garden. Lord Windsor may have been encouraged in this decision by his marriage in 1883 to the beautiful and cosmopolitan Gay Paget, a daughter of Sir Augustus Paget, British Ambassador in Rome.

Lord Windsor (from 1905 the 1st Earl of Plymouth) did not need to worry about the expense of his great undertaking. Together with Hewell he had inherited two other houses, St Fagan's in Glamorganshire and Oakly Park in Shropshire. However, the main source of his wealth was his south Wales estates, centred on Cardiff: he was, with the 3rd Marquess of Bute, a prime beneficiary of the city's nineteenth-century transformation into a great port. His fortune allowed him to build and collect on a princely scale at a time when many of his landed contemporaries were being forced to retrench in the face of the agricultural depression.

Lord Windsor's connoisseurial approach to the creation of his new house was summed up in his decision not to have a contract with its builders, Franklin of Deddington. As he wrote: 'a schedule of prices was agreed upon and the work measured up periodically. Though this plan may not have been an economical one, it was unquestionably the best, as it enabled us to make any alterations as the work proceeded, and it saved us in most cases from the disappointing feeling that if we had had more time to consider details we should have done them differently.'

Although in the 1860s G. F. Bodley had been a pioneer architect of 'Queen Anne' houses, after he went into an informal partnership with Thomas Garner in 1869, he concentrated on church design, leaving domestic commissions largely to his younger partner. Hewell Grange was designed entirely by Garner, and its exterior, crisply executed in pink Runcorn stone, demonstrates a scholarly and sensitive understanding of his sources, most notably Montacute in Somerset. His drawings reveal how the elaborate detail he first proposed was simplified to produce a masterly combination of magnificence and restraint. Garner's first designs for the interiors were Jacobean in spirit, but as Lady Windsor recorded, her husband 'was at that time so imbued with Elizabethan and Italian Renaissance that he requested ... fresh ones.'

Hewell no less than Longleat is a testament to the English love of Italy, but whereas the Marquess of Bath looked principally to High Renaissance Venice for inspiration, Lord Windsor wanted a house that would evoke the more delicate forms of the Quattrocento pictures that he collected. In Hewell's vast living hall the spirit of Brunelleschi is translated into soft English colours: Frosterley marble for the columns, Derbyshire alabaster on the walls and decorative details in Penarth and Italian marbles. Two Bavarian artists, Herr Behr and Herr Virsching, provided painted Renaissance decorative schemes, including, in Lady Windsor's sitting room, a copy in gold and azure of a ceiling in the ducal palace at Mantua. It was an aesthetic setting for an aesthetic couple: Lady Windsor sat for one of Burne-Jones's rare full-length portraits and her husband wrote one of the first scholarly books on Constable. The atmosphere of delicate perfection that they created at Hewell is perfectly captured in William Nicholson's portrait of the family, posed like elegant shadows in the hall.

Hewell Grange was sold by the 3rd Earl of Plymouth in 1946 and many of the contents removed to Oakly Park, Shropshire. It is now an open prison.

The hall in 1902. Although innovatively early-Renaissance Italian in its forms, in plan this great space can be compared with living halls designed by William Burn in the 1840s. As at Sandon Hall, it is divided into three: a staircase hall at the far end, a living hall, and a billiard room, in which the photographer is standing.

STOKESAY COURT, SHROPSHIRE

Stokesay Court is the creation of an elderly man of conventional tastes, who, after a lifetime in trade, wished to establish his family among the landed classes. This involved building and furnishing a new country house on a grand scale. Since money was no object, the result perfectly realized his wishes.

John Derby Allcroft had made an immense fortune as a glove manufacturer. Born in 1822, he followed his father into the Worcester firm of J. and W. Dent & Co., subsequently Dent, Allcroft & Co. Once he became a partner he presided over a great expansion, establishing new headquarters for the firm in the City of London and setting up branches on the Continent and in the USA. In 1873 he took early retirement and at his farewell party he made a gift out of his own pocket to each employee of £10 for every year of their service. It is an indication of the size of both the firm and his fortune that he distributed some £30,000.

By this time, Allcroft had a busy public career, largely centred on his religious interests – he had strong Evangelical views and was sternly opposed to ritualism, an outlook that in 1880 cost him his parliamentary seat in the High Church town of Worcester. He built and endowed three London churches, was a loyal supporter of the Young Men's Christian Association, a prominent Freemason, a governor of Christ's Hospital, and a Fellow of both the Royal Geographical and Royal Astronomical Societies, with a large stuccoed house at 108 Lancaster Gate, Bayswater – in all, the very image of a public-spirited Victorian millionaire.

All that was lacking was the goal of so many prosperous businessmen since the sixteenth century, a country seat. Allcroft set about the creation of one in a characteristically methodical way. In 1869 he purchased the heavily mortgaged Stokesay estate in Shropshire from the Earl of Craven, paying £215,000 for the 5,200 acres. However,

Above: *The garden front of Stokesay Court.*

Right: *The main staircase. The late-nineteenth-century wooden sculptures of young huntsmen are attributed to the Italian sculptor Valentino Besarel.*

there was no house, apart from thirteenth-century Stokesay Castle. It is unlikely that Allcroft ever considered restoring it as a home: not only was it a famously well-preserved medieval manor house, it was also far too small (he did, however, have it sensitively repaired). He steadily enlarged the estate by piecemeal acquisitions, but it was not until 1886 that he was able to buy land near Onibury which provided a good site for a new house: a high wooded ridge, with magnificent views over Ludlow, Clee Hill and the distant Malverns.

In October 1887 Allcroft commissioned Thomas Harris to design a new house, to be called Stokesay Court. Harris is now best remembered for having invented the term 'Victorian architecture' in a pamphlet of 1860 and for campaigning for a new style, to be based on iron, aluminium and terracotta, but if such ideas appealed to Allcroft there is no sign of it at Stokesay. Instead, the house embodies another of Harris's beliefs, that new buildings should be rooted in the native traditions killed by the introduction of Renaissance Classicism – Stokesay is designed in a sturdy late-Elizabethan or early-Jacobean manner. However, Allcroft almost certainly chose his architect not on the basis of his theories, but on his successful record as a designer of country houses, including, only a few miles from Stokesay, Bedstone Court, a pioneering exercise in the half-timbered revival, designed in 1884. Harris also fits into the pattern of Allcroft's architectural patronage, which avoided Gothic revivalists with High Church connections.

The principal contractor was Edward Conder, whose building works were at Baltic Wharf in Kingsland Bridge Road, London. He seems to have satisfied Allcroft just as much as he had Ferdinand Rothschild when building Waddesdon Manor ten years before. The house is built from yellow sandstone quarried on the estate but all the fittings, including the house's handsome and elaborate woodwork, were prefabricated at Baltic Warf and taken by rail to Onibury for assembly on site. The contract for furnishing and decorating the house was won by Hampton & Sons of Pall Mall East, London, who as well as supplying furniture, carpets and textiles also made all the fitted furniture, from chimneypieces to bookshelves. The house was supplied with electric light from the start.

Harris devised a careful architectural progression from the sheer walls and few windows of the entrance court, which faces north west directly into the ridge on which the house is built (see the plan on page 17). Visitors enter a low vestibule, which leads into the double-height, top-lit but rather sombre panelled hall. This makes a dramatic contrast with the airy, light drawing room, decorated in pink, red and white, which looks south over the terrace and gardens, laid out by H. E. Milner in the early 1890s.

Harris was proud of the planning of the house, which observes the usual sharp separation between the main block of the house, for family occupation, and a service court, almost equal in size on plan, attached to its north-east corner. Stokesay embodies also a strong

The central hall. The tall vase in the foreground is part of the large collection of Indian and Burmese artefacts collected by Herbert Allcroft on his extensive foreign travels.

sense of Victorian domestic propriety in the rigid demarcation of male and female living spaces. The Gentlemen's wing, which incorporates a billiard room, card room and business room as well as bachelors' bedrooms, is on the west side of the main house, as far away as possible from the Ladies' wing on the south side of the service court. This distinction is reinforced in the decoration: dark anaglyptas and Japanese gilt papers for the men's rooms; white-painted furniture and pink silk upholstery for the ladies.

These rooms formed the setting for a large collection of pictures formed by Allcroft. He was very fond of the pastoral scenes of Thomas Sidney Cooper – in 1873 he paid £2,500 for his enormous canvas *The Monarch of the Meadows*, a depiction of a mighty bull, which was hung over the stairs – but most of the artists are now less well known: Thomas Musgrove Joy, George Cole, Charles Lidderdale, Erskine Nicol and John Morgan. Most regularly showed works at the Royal Academy or the Royal Society of British Artists in Suffolk Street, so it is easy to imagine Allcroft making his annual visit to their exhibitions, chequebook in hand.

When work was finished, in 1892, Allcroft calculated that he had spent £101,814 building the house. If the cost of acquiring the estate is added to this, he had laid out nearly £500,000 on the creation of his country seat. Allcroft died the following year, bequeathing the estate to his eldest son, Herbert, who had been groomed for the life of a country gentleman.

In 1950, Stokesay was inherited by Herbert's daughter Jewell, who had married the historian Sir Philip Magnus. They had no children and on her death in 1992 Lady Magnus-Allcroft divided her estate between three beneficiaries, including a nephew and niece. Stokesay's significance as an intact late-Victorian country house was swiftly recognized, but the National Heritage Memorial Fund refused to support English Heritage's attempt to acquire the house for the nation, and its contents were sold at auction in 1994. However, Lady Magnus-Allcroft's niece, Caroline Magnus, retained a small part of the contents and continues to live in the house.

Above: *The drawing room. The only major element that has been lost from this exceptionally well-preserved interior is the 'paper to special shades' that the decorators, Hampton & Sons, used in panels on the walls.*

Right: *The drawing room's chimneypiece, one of the fittings designed by the house's architect, Thomas Harris.*

WADDESDON MANOR, BUCKINGHAMSHIRE

Many estate villages proclaim their ownership in the name of their inn – at Baslow in Derbyshire, for example, the Devonshire Arms is an early clue that a visitor has arrived on the Chatsworth estate. The inn at Waddesdon, the Five Arrows, multi-gabled and tile-hung, with tall, twisting Tudor brick chimneys, at once suggests Victorian affluence of an unusual kind. Its name, however, may not immediately reveal the source of that money unless a visitor knows that there are five arrows on the Rothschild coat of arms. They commemorate the five brothers who, after an upbringing in the Frankfurt ghetto, established a family bank in the city with branches in Paris, Vienna, London and Naples. It rapidly became one of the financial powerhouses of nineteenth-century Europe, having seized the opportunities offered by the Napoleonic Wars, which forced governments to raise unprecedented sums of money from banks in order to finance their campaigns.

The English arrow was Nathan, who settled in London in 1811. He lived in comfortable suburban circumstances at Gunnersbury, west London, but in the late 1840s and early 1850s all three of his sons purchased country estates in Buckinghamshire, which was conveniently accessible from London by railway and offered good sport – although anti-Semitism kept the Rothschilds out of the local hunts, they set up their own pack of stag hounds. Land was also essential as a basis for political influence; in 1847 Nathan's eldest son, Lionel, became the first practising Jew to be elected to parliament. Nathan's youngest son, Mayer, acquired an estate at Mentmore which had no suitable accommodation, so he built there one of the great houses of the age. Begun in 1851, Mentmore Towers was designed by

Above: *The garden front of Waddesdon Manor, which overlooks a formal parterre.*

Left: *The entrance front, photographed in 1902. The main house was completed in 1882. The morning room wing on the right, partly concealed by the tree, was added in 1889–91.*

G. H. Stokes and his father-in-law, Joseph Paxton, to resemble one of the great houses of Elizabethan England.

Nathan also had a daughter, Charlotte, who in 1826 married her cousin Anselm, son of the brother who had founded the Vienna bank. In the nineteenth century Rothschilds almost always married within their family. They strongly disapproved of marriages outside their Jewish faith, and there were very few Jewish families who could even approach their rank or wealth. Charlotte and Anselm's seven children enjoyed a life that was cosmopolitan as well as plutocratic: Jews were not able to own property in Austria and so the family divided their time between a townhouse in Paris, a small estate just outside Frankfurt and a large country house, Schillersdorf, in Silesia.

Above: *The Grey Drawing Room. Its panelling was taken from a Parisian townhouse of 1728–32 (now the Musée Rodin). The room is furnished with a Savonnerie carpet and chairs covered with Beauvais tapestry, mixed with comfortable modern upholstered pieces.*

Left: *The dining room, which is lined with marble and hung with a series of Beauvais tapestries after Boucher. The mirror frames, designed by Nicolas Pineal in 1732–33, are from the Paris house of the duc de Villas. They are part of a set of fourteen, of which the remainder are in Mentmore Towers, the home of Ferdinand's uncle, Mayer de Rothschild.*

Their youngest son, Ferdinand, who was particularly close to his mother, was much distressed by her early death, in 1859. Shortly afterwards he decided to make his home permanently in England, and in 1865 married one of his English cousins, Evelina. Barely eighteen months after their wedding, Evelina died giving birth to a still-born child. Ferdinand was grief-stricken; he never remarried.

A member of the first generation of Rothschilds who were not compelled to work in the bank, Ferdinand had no interest in business. On the modest allowance that Anselm granted him, he occupied himself with travel and with helping his uncles in their pursuit of works of art, for the Rothschild tradition of collecting was already well established. Ferdinand's personality was a mixture of nervous anxiety and energy as well as great charm; he was held in amused affection by his worldly English cousins, whose social ease he desperately tried to imitate.

Then in 1874 Anselm died, dividing his share in the bank between his three sons. Ferdinand at once asked to liquidate his assets, for virtually within days of hearing of his father's death he had bought an estate in Buckinghamshire from the Duke of Marlborough.

The £170,000 he paid was a high price – and was soon to seem even higher when land values fell in the following decade – especially as there was no large house there. Although the traditional centre of the estate was at Winchendon, Ferdinand called the estate Waddesdon from the start, as he had decided to build a new mansion at the top of a steep hill, just outside that village. His family was astonished by the challenge he had taken on, but for Ferdinand the bare, muddy, inaccessible fields were just the blank canvas that he required.

For the next five years a huge team of labourers under the control of the main contractor, Edward Conder of London, toiled to level the top of the hill and to create a drive winding up to its summit. This long delay gave Ferdinand the opportunity to refine the designs for the house, which he had commissioned soon after he had bought the estate. His architect was a Frenchman, Gabriel-Hippolyte Destailleur, who was based in Paris. Ferdinand explained that his choice of designer was governed by his decision to have a house in a French Renaissance style. He claimed that the idea had come to him during a tour of the Loire châteaux, but a more likely explanation is the Rothschilds' close and competitive interest in each others' collecting and commissioning. By choosing a French style for Waddesdon, Ferdinand avoided comparisons being made with the Rothschilds' other Buckinghamshire houses, notably Mentmore.

In Destailleur, a considerable scholar of historic French architecture, he had an architect who was able to create just the sort of smooth synthesis of French Renaissance models – Chambord, Blois, Chaumont and so on – that he had envisaged. The essential idea for the house – based on Schillersdorf – of a long, thin building with all the major rooms looking south over the vale of Aylesbury was there from the beginning. However, Destailleur originally proposed raising the house on a high basement, apparently to contain service quarters, but his second design revised this to the more normal plan of a separate service court. Ferdinand also made him reduce the scale of the house, against his architect's advice – 'one always builds too small.' The result of these decisions is a comparatively low house, with an almost clotted richness of ornament, which composes better from a distance than it does close up.

Destailleur provided designs for fireplaces and other fittings. Thanks to his busy practice in Paris he was also able to let Ferdinand know when fine *boiseries* suitable for Waddesdon came onto the market. There is a myth that the house benefited from the demolitions ordered by Napoleon III in the 1870s to create Paris's boulevards, but in fact almost every house from which Ferdinand obtained his panelling still stands. He claimed that his family was the first to create complete interiors out of 'old materials', apparently unaware of the long tradition of the use of such salvage in English country houses, but there is little doubt that very few houses can compare with Waddesdon in the harmony with which these elements were combined into modern interiors.

The East Gallery, hung with two enormous views of Venice by Francesco Guardi and fitted out with eighteenth-century French panelling.

This was almost entirely Ferdinand's achievement. He did not follow the customary practice of contracting out the decoration and furnishing, preferring to rely on his eye alone, not only when acquiring his great treasures of eighteenth-century French furniture, porcelain, bronzes and textiles, but also when arranging them. The luxury and expense of what he created is embodied in such wonderfully extravagant touches as the use of Savonnerie stool covers from the chapel at Versailles as hearthrugs – but what is far less often appreciated is the aesthetic quality and control of the ensemble.

Soon after the house was finished, in 1882, Ferdinand recognized that Destailleur was right and that he had built too small, as there was no room large enough for all his guests to assemble in during the day. Destailleur returned at the end of the 1880s to add a large new morning room on the west end of the house, and at the same time Ferdinand extended the accommodation for bachelors at its east end, which included a smoking room and a billiard room fitted out in Renaissance style. Guests were accommodated in great comfort, and treated rather as they would have been in one of London's or New York's new luxury hotels. Entertaining was Waddesdon's real purpose and it was used for only five months of the year – for summer house parties and shooting in the autumn.

On Ferdinand's death in 1898, the house was inherited by his unmarried sister Alice, who owned the neighbouring estate of Eythrope. She bequeathed Waddesdon in 1922 to her French cousin James de Rothschild. In 1957 he left the house, its contents and gardens to the National Trust with a large endowment under the control of independent trustees, who included his widow, Dorothy. When she died in 1988, the estate and the controlling hand on the endowment passed to her cousin, Jacob Rothschild, from 1990 the 4th Lord Rothschild. He undertook a comprehensive restoration of the house and garden, and has added significantly to Waddesdon's collections.

Above: *The smoking room, designed to house Ferdinand's medieval and Renaissance* objets d'art. *By the time this photograph was taken, in 1902, his collection had been removed, as he had bequeathed it to the British Museum, but the objects collected for the room by his sister and heir, Alice, give some idea of its original glamour.*

Right: *The chimneypiece in the billiard room. The stone overmantel was carved in France in the late sixteenth century.*

FIVE ARROWS HOTEL
18 87
Hotel

Although the country houses commissioned by the Rothschilds for the network of seven estates that they built up in the Vale of Aylesbury between the 1840s and 1870s were in a variety of styles – Classical, Jacobean and French Renaissance – their very extensive estate buildings were almost all designed in an English vernacular manner. The style was set by Sir Anthony de Rothschild on his Aston Clinton estate when in 1863 he employed George Devey, a pioneer of the vernacular revival, to design a pair of schools. Devey went on to work for almost all the Rothschilds, notably for Mayer de Rothschild at Mentmore. At Waddesdon, however, Ferdinand Rothschild employed a local architect, W. F. Taylor of Bierton, for estate buildings, but they were firmly in the idiom that Devey had created.

ROTHSCHILD ESTATE BUILDINGS This page (top left): *The school at Hulcott, remodelled in 1864 by George Devey for Sir Anthony de Rothschild;* (top right): *The Club and Reading Room at Waddesdon, by W. F. Taylor, 1883;* (below left): *The South Lodge, Mentmore, by George Devey for Mayer de Rothschild, 1868;* (below right): *Sgrafitto decoration on a cottage in Halton, commissioned by Alfred de Rothschild in the 1880s.*

Left: *The Five Arrows Hotel at Waddesdon, by W. F. Taylor, 1887.*

6
7
5
8
4
9
3
10
2
1
12
11
Decus angelrū
Glria i excels
To no one is given
Right of delay,
Noted in heaven,
Passeth each day
Be not thou fruitless;
Work while ye may
Trifling were bootless
Watch thou and pray

1890

SEDUCTIVE IMAGES

In 1801 four-fifths of the population of the British Isles lived in the countryside; when Queen Victoria died, exactly a century later, four-fifths lived in cities and towns. This was the background to the idealization of rural existence that had become such a potent force in British culture by the end of the nineteenth century. Few people reading *Country Life*, launched in 1897, would have gleaned from it much sense of the demoralization and depression of the rural economy. For the magazine's readers, the countryside was primarily a place for sport and relaxation, and the centre of such activities was the country house. Especially in counties within easy reach of London, where most of the magazine's readers lived, such houses, now almost entirely divorced from their agricultural origins, could be bought and restored at no great expense, furnished and decorated with taste, and provided with a new garden.

If no sufficiently attractive old house were available, then there were plenty of architects able to create new ones that were scarcely less beguiling. But for all that they often contained large service wings and numerous guest rooms, such houses looked back not to the architectural traditions of the great house, but to the rapidly eroding traditional forms and crafts of the English countryside. This was an idea that goes back to Richard Norman Shaw's creation of the 'Old English' style in the late 1860s, but younger architects in the 1890s, such as W. R. Lethaby, hankered for something less self-evidently in the service of the rich. Their hero was William Morris's old friend Philip Webb, who in such houses as Standen revealed a strong streak of puritanism, which was a reaction against the luxury and conspicuous expenditure so evident in English society at the end of the century.

However, most patrons preferred more obvious visual enticement than Webb was willing to provide. It now seems hard to believe that a house such as Old Place had a real existence outside the pages of *Country Life*, and it does not come as a surprise to learn that its creator, C. E. Kempe, was a designer of stained glass and interiors rather than an architect. Yet, as at Wood House, Essex, he was responsible for buildings of seductive beauty of a type that – thanks in part to the genius of such photographers as Charles Latham – influenced the tastes of early-twentieth-century Britain (and America) far more extensively than the Arts and Crafts movement.

Webb and Kempe were divergent strands in late-Victorian country-house design, but they shared a common distaste for most of what had been distinctive about Victorian country houses. Everything they disliked was epitomized by what may well be regarded as the last Victorian country house, since it was finished in the year that Edward VII ascended the throne. A confident fusion of a scholarly recreation of medieval forms with the latest technology, Arundel Castle is a deeply impressive embodiment of the sense of social and religious responsibility evident in so many of the great Victorian houses. It sums up a tradition that barely survived the reign in which it was created.

A sundial in stained glass made by C. E. Kempe's company for his house, Old Place, Lindfield, Sussex.

OLD PLACE, LINDFIELD, SUSSEX

Country Life's early photographers had a remarkable gift for creating poetic compositions. However, in the case of Old Place their task was made easier by a house that seems to have been designed especially for the camera. It is not surprising that the architect G. F. Bodley described its rooms as a 'series of pictures'; they look ravishing in the large-format plates by Charles Latham, illustrating the four articles that the magazine devoted to this 'most beautiful and artistic abode' between 1900 and 1907. 'Ask yourself', wrote C. J. Cornish in 1900, 'if anything can be more English in character than the Old Place.' Yet most of the house was then barely a decade old.

Old Place sits in large grounds near the parish church in Lindfield, even now a very picturesque village, north east of Hayward's Heath. The original house, tall, timber-framed and brick-nogged, dates mostly from around 1590. In 1875 it was bought by Charles Eamer Kempe, one of the most celebrated stained-glass designers and manufacturers of the late nineteenth century, who had recently received a substantial inheritance from his mother. He had been born plain Charles Kemp in 1837, a member of a large, prosperous family who had been lords of the manor in Brighton, where their name is commemorated in Kemp Town, a development of the 1820s on land that they owned. A bad stammer prevented Kemp from entering the Church as he had wished, and so on the advice of G. F. Bodley, whose family lived in Brighton, he studied stained-glass design with Clayton & Bell. In 1869 – by when he had changed his name to Kempe – he set up his own firm in London, which, under Bodley's influence, specialized in the recent turn in ecclesiastical fashion to late-medieval English and North European models, and emphasized refinement of draughtsmanship and delicacy of colour.

Right: *The garden front dominated by a tall sundial. Kempe laid out the elaborate formal garden in the 1890s after completing his new wing.*

Below: *The entrance to Old Place, showing the original, Elizabethan house.*

NVNC SOL
NVNC VMBRA

In some ways the purchase of Old Place is typical of the way that numerous well-off late-Victorian businessmen bought and restored picturesque old manor houses within easy reach of London or other big cities. Few, however, attempted to create such aesthetic harmony, which was designed not as a family home – Kempe never married – but as a backdrop to entertaining. In 1890 he decided to extend the house with a substantial south wing. The drawings, modelled on another Tudor house in Lindfield, East Mascalls, were by William Tate, an architect employed by Kempe's firm, but the design was presumably in essence Kempe's. The foundation stone was laid by Frances Wolseley, daughter of his friend Lady Wolseley, wife of a celebrated general, Garnet Wolseley, and a noted collector of old furniture. Lady Wolseley's description of the ceremony in a letter to her husband captures the spirit of life at Old Place: 'We had such a pretty little simple ceremony, all standing round the foundations in the garden – *all* being only we and three-and-twenty workmen. We stood on lovely Indian rugs, the workmen bare-headed, Frances smoothed the mortar and tapped the stone and said *Floreat Domus*, putting a new coin under the stone. Mr Kempe made a little speech explaining *Floreat Domus*, and saying that, begun by good workmen, it must flourish. Then we all sang "God Save the Queen". Then we drank a loving-cup and the workmen after us. It was a nice brown crockery three-handled tankard and replenished from an old copper "black Jack" shaped jug, with a bunch of borage in it. (I am sure he knew the blue of the borage would look well in the copper).'

All the descriptions of the house emphasize that the new work seamlessly blended with the old, but, as Cornish wrote in *Country Life* in 1900, when visitors moved from the original house to the new wing, they passed 'from what was good but modest in calibre … into something great and ennobled in the reign of Queen Victoria.' He perceptively analyzed the way that Kempe had blended medieval carvings from Germany with old English furniture, Turkish rugs and

Above: *The Great Parlour, described by C. J. Cornish in* Country Life *in 1900 as 'a mediaeval hall developed to its artistic conclusion'.*

Left: *The dining room, in Old Place's 1890 wing.*

modern stained glass and plasterwork, singling out the dining room for special praise: 'the ancient hangings on the walls of this fine room are of a green tint, against which large silver sconces shine, and foliage tapestry scarcely distinguishable from ancient examples, but recently woven in the looms of France, testifies to the skill of the modern weaver when working under the educating influences of the student in ancient art.'

Not everyone warmed to such interiors, particularly as Kempe, who was inclined to be touchy and querulous, struck many people as affected. The waspish diarist A. C. Benson, a close neighbour, enjoyed Kempe's hospitality but disliked what he saw as the flaunting of his wealth and dogmatism about art and design. He thought these aspects of his personality were reflected in the increasingly repetitive and formulaic nature of his stained glass, in which, Benson wrote in 1903, all the figures looked like Kempe himself: 'We do *not* want unadulterated Kempe everywhere. We don't want Mr Kempe as St Peter, only bleached like celery, without the wholesome oranges and purples of Mr K's face – talking to Mr K as St Andrew – with two Mr Kempes talking in the distance; and Mary Magdalene (as Mr Kempe shaved and feminised) falling to the ground under a weight of Turkey carpets.'

It is hard not to agree with Benson's view of Kempe's later stained glass (almost none of which he designed himself) while still regretting the dispersal of the contents of Old Place. Kempe died in 1907, bequeathing the house to the architect Walter Tower, a distant cousin, who succeeded Kempe as chairman of the firm. Tower sold Old Place in 1925; it survives, but has been subdivided.

Above: *The Dial Room, a combination of eighteenth-century English furniture and Turkish carpets with modern plasterwork imitating seventeenth-century models.*

Right: *A bay window, filled with glass in Renaissance style designed by Kempe and made by his firm.*

AVON TYRRELL, HAMPSHIRE

Nobody who has visited Cragside can forget its stupendous drawing-room chimneypiece, designed by one of Norman Shaw's most talented assistants, W. R. Lethaby (see pages 120–21). A major figure in the Arts and Crafts movement, Lethaby was a founding member of one of its key organizations, the Art Workers' Guild, and a dedicated participant in William Morris's Society for the Protection of Ancient Buildings, where he became a good friend of Philip Webb (whose biography he was to write). When a friend referred to Lethaby as one of Shaw's pupils, Shaw replied, 'No, on the contrary it is I who am Lethaby's pupil.' This admiration was translated into practical help in 1889, when, at the age of thirty-two, Lethaby decided to set up his own practice. Shaw passed on to him a plum commission, the design of a new country house on the edge of the New Forest, near Christchurch, for the 3rd Baron Manners.

Lord Manners was the grandson of Thomas Manners-Sutton, a successful lawyer who was raised to the peerage in 1807 when he was appointed Lord Chancellor of Ireland. They were not a landed family, and Avon Tyrrell was built on an estate owned by the family of Lord Manners's wife, Constance Fane, whom he had married in 1885. The couple have an interesting history of artistic patronage: in 1896 their eldest son was the subject of one of Millais' last portraits, showing the boy dressed in Regency costume as though posed by Lawrence, and in 1906 Lord Manners commissioned not only another major building, Detmar Blow's All Saints' church at Thorney Hill, Hampshire, but also its magnificent murals by the Irish-born Arts and Crafts artist Phoebe Traquair.

Lengthy correspondence between Lethaby and Lord Manners charts the careful working out of the house's plan. Their discussions resulted in a complex, austerely detailed entrance front and a simpler but more festive garden front, where the principal feature is, in Lethaby's words, 'a series of Bay windows which would both catch the morning sun and command the view.' The only serious

Right: *The garden front. In the distance is a summer house designed by W. R. Lethaby.*

Below: *Avon Tyrrell, seen across its entrance courtyard. The large window to the right of the front door lights the hall. Note the peacocks on the gables.*

disagreement occurred over the placing of the nurseries, which Lethaby, perhaps with an Arts and Crafts idealization of family life, wanted to put on the principal bedroom floor. With difficulty Lady Manners persuaded him to transfer them to the more customary position of the attic storey.

The interiors reveal Lethaby's lyrical gift for decoration. The plasterwork, of coiled and budding foliage in low relief, was designed and executed under his guidance by Ernest Gimson. In 1890 Lethaby and Gimson set up Kenton & Co. to supply 'furniture of good design and good workmanship'. *Country Life*'s photograph of the hall at Avon Tyrrell shows a table supplied by Kenton & Co. that was almost certainly designed by Lethaby. More idiosyncratic was the striking use of coloured stones for interior decoration, perhaps influenced by Lethaby's deep interest in Byzantine art. The extraordinary hall chimneypiece was praised by Lawrence Weaver in *Country Life* for its 'perception of the beauty of large, smooth coloured surfaces, patterned on lines of fresh severity. Green marble and Hopton Wood stone with its cool grey-brown tones make a gentle contrast very pleasant to look at.'

Weaver was less sure about another striking feature: the stone peacocks that perch on the little gables above the front door. They have a heraldic function – the peacock is the Manners crest – but (as emblems of immortality) also recall Lethaby's interest in architectural symbolism, the subject of his first book, *Architecture, Mysticism, and Myth*, published in 1891. 'These birds have an air of acquaintance with Noah's Ark', wrote Weaver, adding, 'they are an experiment which it would not be wise for others, less certain of themselves to follow.' Lethaby certainly did not lack self-confidence, insisting that control over the garden layout was left to him and not entrusted to the celebrated landscape designer H. E. Milner, whom Lord Manners had employed for the task.

In 1946 the 4th Lord Manners presented Avon Tyrrell to the nation for the use of young people. It is now a youth activity centre for the New Forest.

Above: *The hall, looking towards the screens passage.*

Left: *The hall chimneypiece, an exercise in abstract composition in green and grey.*

STANDEN, SUSSEX

By the time that he designed Standen, in 1891, Philip Webb was revered by younger architects as a founding father of the Arts and Crafts movement. Yet his reputation was not based on publicity, as almost none of his houses were published until *Country Life* photographed several for articles by Lawrence Weaver in the early twentieth century. This was not in itself unusual: William Burn, George Devey and many other nineteenth-century architects specializing in country houses were similarly discreet, largely out of respect for their clients' privacy. But Webb was reticent also in his approach to design. The only justification for a house drawing attention to itself, he believed, was the quality of its building and craftsmanship; any idea that it might suggest 'style', either in terms of historical precedent or an architect's personality, was anathema. Yet Webb's artistic taciturnity was allied to an iron will: according to one of his assistants, George Jack, 'If clients questioned, he used persuasion; and if that failed he recommended them to try another architect. In his office-work every detail was designed by himself, to the smallest moulding.'

Webb's clients at Standen, James and Margaret Beale, had a taste of this intransigence at the outset. In 1890 they had bought three farms in the rolling wooded landscape of the Sussex Weald, a few miles south of East Grinstead, intending to build a house for their retirement. They commissioned the garden designer G. B. Simpson to select and landscape a site, so when Webb paid his first visit to Standen, in April 1891, he discovered that the Beales had already at some expense levelled the proposed plot. As Jack recalled, 'Webb made up his mind to put the house some yards away from the

Above: *The entrance front. Webb added the hall's bay window, on the right of the front door, in 1898, to accommodate a piano.*

Right: *The garden front. The long conservatory to the left of the main block is part of Webb's original design.*

proposed position. This meant a great change of entrance-way, &c., and shocked Mr Beale, but when the house was built – indeed, before it was finished – he expressed his satisfaction.' Beale and his wife recalled this incident in the gift they made to Webb when the house was completed in 1894 – a snuffbox inscribed, 'When clients talk irritating nonsense I take a pinch of snuff.'

James and Margaret Beale both came from prosperous Birmingham Non-Conformist families with a long tradition of civic service. He was a solicitor whose family firm received so much work from the Midland Railway that it was decided that he should open a London office. In the late 1870s he and his family – there were three sons and three daughters – settled in Holland Park, which had been made fashionable by artists and writers. It is not known how the Beales came to choose Webb as their architect for Standen, but they may have been aware of his work for their neighbour Alexander Ionides, a financier, whose house was redecorated in 1880 by Morris & Co. under Webb's supervision. They were surely aware of his links with Morris, a close friend of Webb since 1856, when he was an assistant in G. E. Street's office and Morris was briefly a pupil.

As a result of Webb insisting on Standen's site being moved, so that it sat more tightly in the angle of a low ridge, it was impossible to build an approach straight from the road to its entrance front. Instead the drive first winds round a large, open grassed space, like a village green. Here Webb preserved not only the red-brick, tile-hung farm buildings, but also the existing trees. The approach then dives through a narrow gateway into the entrance court, dominated by a low, squat water tower, which acts as the pivot between the two wings, the service range on the west and the main house on the south.

Above: *The drawing room, hung as originally with Morris's 'Sunflower' wallpaper. The copper, electric wall lights were designed by Webb and made by John Pearson. The easy chair to the right of the fireplace and the 'Chippendale' settee in the alcove were made by Morris & Co.*

Left: *The chimneypiece in the hall. The hanging light fittings, designed by W. A. S. Benson, were installed in 1894. Their opalescent shades were made by Powell of Whitefriars.*

The house's principal façade, which looks out over the gardens to the Ashdown Forest, is crowned by a row of five, high, weather-boarded gables. As W. R. Lethaby noted in his biography of the architect, published in 1935, 'a series of gables like so many waves always appealed to Webb'. Most of the materials of the house take their cue from the site's existing buildings: local limestone, red Keymer bricks, clay tiles and oak shingles, combined with roughcast render for the tower and Portland stone for window sills and other elements vulnerable to weather damage. Carefully avoiding any suggestion of 'period' detail, Webb manipulated these materials with such a beguiling variety of detail that the larger composition is at times almost lost sight of.

The interior was treated with great simplicity, with most of the rooms panelled and painted white or hung with Morris papers. However, Webb gave them variety with a remarkable range of chimneypieces, many of which are ingenious extensions of the panelling. The Beales chose chintzes and embroidered textiles from Morris & Co. and bought furniture from a range of fashionable designers, including Agnes and Rhoda Garrett and Collinson & Lock, as well as Morris. From the start Standen was lit by electricity. Webb designed copper sconces made by John Pearson, senior metal-worker at C. R. Ashbee's Guild of Handicraft; Pearson also made the *repoussé* metal cheeks for the drawing room and dining-room chimneypieces. Other light fittings were designed and made by W. A. S. Benson, who became managing director of Morris & Co. after Morris died.

Country Life returned to photograph the house in 1970, at the end of its time as a private house. In 1972 it was bequeathed to the National Trust by James and Margaret Beale's last surviving child, Helen. The Trust was able to accept it without a large endowment when Arthur and Helen Grogan offered to pay a generous sum for a long lease. The house is used to display their important collection of Arts and Crafts design, notably ceramics, enhancing yet further Standen's international celebrity as a place of pilgrimage for admirers of Webb and the Arts and Crafts movement.

Above: *The billiard room. Originally wallpapered, the room was panelled in 1907 to a design by Webb's former assistant, George Jack.*

Right: *The bay in the dining room. Unlike most of the house, where the panelling was painted white, this room has always been painted greeny-blue, partly to set off a display of blue-and-white china. The fitted dressers were designed by Webb.*

WOOD HOUSE, ESSEX

If one had to choose a house that could have served as the setting for *The Spoils of Poynton*, then Wood House, designed in 1897, the year in which Henry James's novel appeared in book form, would have been an ideal candidate. It was, like Poynton, a miniature palace of art, filled with a fine collection of art and antique furniture, arranged with fastidious taste. Moreover, its history was closely entwined with another house that, like Poynton, was destroyed by fire.

In 1869 George Wythes, who had made a fortune as a railway contractor, bought the Copped Hall estate near Epping as a country seat for his only son, George. In 1887 it was inherited by the younger George's son, Ernest Wythes. Two years later, his grandfather died, leaving him a substantial inheritance. His first act on leaving university was to buy a steam yacht, the *St George*, in which – accompanied by seven friends, a crew of forty-eight and a harmonium for Sunday worship (he was High Church) – he sailed round the world. On his return he set about extending Copped Hall, a substantial mid-eighteenth-century house, and commissioned Charles Eamer Kempe to redecorate the interiors and lay out a large new garden in an Italian Renaissance style. Kempe was an unusual choice for such a project, as he was best known as a stained-glass artist and church decorator, but, as his own house, Old Place at Lindfield, Sussex, revealed, he had a gift for creating picturesque interiors designed to show off collections of art and furniture. It seems likely that he was introduced to Wythes by the architect G. F. Bodley, with whom Kempe had been associated since the 1860s. In 1889 Bodley had been commissioned to design a new parish church for Epping, St John's, to which Ernest Wythes contributed generously.

In 1894 Wythes married Aline Thorold, a daughter of Sir John Thorold, Bt. Three years later they commissioned a new house on the

Above: *The entrance court. Because the ground falls away steeply to the garden, the house is entered at first-floor level.*

Right: *The garden front. The garden, laid out formally with trimmed yews and avenues of limes, was designed by C. E. Kempe and Walter Tower.*

edge of the estate for one of her mother's brothers, the Hon. Harry Willoughby, a son of the 8th Lord Middleton. The architect was Walter Tower, a distant cousin of Kempe (and his eventual heir), but the guiding hand in the design was evidently Kempe's. The house is set into a steep ridge, which means that the entrance court is at first-floor level, making the loftiness of the garden front unexpected. The four pargetted, lattice-windowed bays that overlook the formal garden are derived from a historic model much loved by late-nineteenth-century architects, the picturesque seventeenth-century façade of Sparrows House in Ipswich. The principal rooms are on the first floor; the garden floor's smaller rooms included a study and a chapel.

Harry Willoughby barely had time to enjoy the house, as he died aged only fifty-one in 1900. However, Wood House was given a new purpose when in 1917 Copped Hall was gutted by fire. Ernest and Aline Wythes decided to move into Wood House while Copped Hall was rebuilt, and they furnished it with the collections rescued from the flames. In the event, Copped Hall was left a ruin, as it remains (although a private trust has now embarked on its restoration).

Tower's designs for the house reveal that he was asked by the Wythes to scale down his original proposals; he subsequently had some difficulty keeping within the budget that they had set. The contractors were Norman and Burt of Burgess Hill, Sussex, who also worked for Kempe at Old Place; the very fine Neo-Jacobean plaster-work was carried out by Battiscombe and Harris of New Cavendish Street, London. Kempe supplied stained glass for the drawing-room windows. The rooms that resulted were the setting for considerable treasures: gold-ground Italian paintings, fifteenth-century Flemish panel pictures, seventeenth-century tapestries and lacquered Chinese cabinets, *blanc-de-chine* porcelain, Elizabethan portraits, and paintings by Van de Capelle, Reynolds and other Old Masters.

On Ernest Wythes's death in 1949, the house was inherited by his daughter Barbara, who was married to the architect Guy Elwes. *Country Life*'s photographs, taken in 1959, record the house as it appeared shortly before they sold it, with Ernest Wythes's collections still in place. Mark Girouard's article brilliantly evoked its atmosphere: 'The light, somewhat muted by heavy curtains and stained glass, lit up rich tapestries, brocades and carpets. Most of the furniture was carved, inlaid or lacquered; fine pictures hung in heavy gold frames; there was a multitude of porcelain figures, vases, snuff-boxes and all the other objects with which that age liked to sprinkle its shelves and tables. Not much of the contents of the house dated from later than the 18th century, for the contemporary furniture and fittings of Morris, Godwin and Voysey penetrated to few upper-class homes. Yet the Wood House was far removed from the conventional period-furnished house of to-day. It was bathed in a kind of golden glow of wealth, taste and security; it seemed to form the visual equivalent of Henry James's leisured and intricate prose.'

The drawing room, in which the plasterwork and panelling, designed by Kempe and Tower, formed the perfect backdrop for Ernest Wythes's collection of paintings, furniture and porcelain. The seventeenth-century chimneypiece was installed in about 1930 in place of the 1898 original.

ARUNDEL CASTLE, SUSSEX

George Gilbert Scott's dismay that the Duke of Northumberland chose to combine a Gothic exterior with Renaissance interiors at Alnwick would have turned to joy at the sight of Arundel Castle. The seat of the Dukes of Norfolk is not simply the biggest Gothic Revival house in England; it is Gothic to its last keyhole. It was designed by Charles Alban Buckler for Henry Fitzalan-Howard, 15th Duke of Norfolk. Together they pored over books on thirteenth-century architecture in search of precedents that could be adapted for kitchen cupboards, electric-light fittings, picture hooks and even a billiard table. But by the time that the castle was completed, in 1901, Scott had been dead for twenty-three years, and his hope that Gothic would become the style of the nineteenth century had long been abandoned. How is it that so pure an exercise in the Gothic Revival should have been built decades after architects had rejected it for domestic purposes? The explanation is that the Duke's vision of a new Gothic house was formed when he came of age in 1868, but its realization was delayed by family tragedy.

The 15th Duke inherited a building of great complexity. At its heart is a twelfth-century shell keep, crowning a motte a century older, but the habitable parts of the castle are arranged around a long, large courtyard to its south. In 1718, the 8th Duke patched up the ruins left by the Civil War, but Arundel was used only occasionally for most of the eighteenth century, as the family's principal country house was Worksop Manor in Nottinghamshire. Then, in 1791, the 11th Duke undertook a major campaign of rebuilding, to create a series of state rooms in the south range and a new great hall in the west range. All was Norman or Gothic, and elaborate in conception, since the Duke intended Arundel to resume its historic role as the main family seat. His successors added a suite of family rooms in the east wing and then a large chapel to the north of the great hall.

Above: *A distant view of Arundel Castle from the east, photographed in 1991: the medieval keep is on the right, the Victorian additions on the left.*

Right: *The dramatic silhouette of the west wing, built in 1893–98.*

When the 15th Duke took control of his estates after an eight-year minority, he at once revealed his intention to be an architectural patron on a grand scale. In 1869 he commissioned J. A. Hansom to design a church for Arundel that would proudly proclaim the Roman Catholicism to which the Fitzalan-Howards had remained loyal since the Reformation. This majestic building, on the scale of a small cathedral (which is what it became) was completed in 1873. The Duke then turned his attention to the castle, determined to fuse its disparate parts into a harmonious whole. The architect he chose came from an Oxford family with a long tradition of art and antiquarian scholarship: C. A. Buckler's father was John Chessell Buckler, a well-known topographical artist. Steeped in the study of medieval architecture, he began work by visiting ancient Sussex castles, such as Bodiam and Pevensey.

Above: *The drawing room. This is the principal state room completed by Buckler before work was interrupted in the 1880s by the Duchess's illness. The chimneypiece, carved by Thomas Earp, displays the arms of the 15th Duke impaled with those of his first wife.*

Left: *The chapel in 1914: a view from its north aisle into the nave.*

The Duke wished to retain the convenient layout of the family rooms and state apartments, and so Buckler was able only to reface the east and south wings, but the great hall and chapel, on the west, failed to live up to late-Victorian scholarly ideals of Gothic design and the Duke decided to demolish them. Work started in 1877 with the family rooms, but before the new west wing could be begun, the Duke was distracted by domestic grief. In 1877 he had married Lady Flora Abney-Hastings, and two years later their only child, Philip, was born. Tragically, he was brain-damaged, blind and epileptic, but with his parents' care survived, and lived to be twenty-one. The Duchess's health declined and she died in 1887, aged only thirty-four. While she was ill the Duke suspended building at Arundel, but after her death took it up on an even greater scale than originally planned, partly as a solace in bereavement (he did not remarry until 1904).

Buckler gave the castle a much bolder and more convincingly medieval silhouette, but the Duke was not solely interested in creating a vision of the Gothic past. He was equally concerned to harness all the benefits of modern technology. At his suggestion, the windows were fitted with casements of gun metal rather than iron, to avoid corrosion; almost none of the castle's exterior requires painting, avoiding problems with maintenance. The castle was lit by electricity, installed in 1891–99; it had eight bathrooms and sixty-five WCs, central heating, integral fire-fighting equipment and hydraulically powered service lifts.

Nonetheless, the main interiors created in the 1890s – the dining room, chapel and Baron's Hall – are overpoweringly medieval in conception. The most extraordinary is the enormous dining room, 60 feet long and 34 feet high. Its ecclesiastical atmosphere is not accidental: the Duke first intended it to be his new chapel. The three great lancet windows were inserted by Buckler in the 1870s, but nothing more was done during the Duchess's illness. When building resumed in the 1890s the Duke decided to build an even bigger chapel on the site of the one added earlier in the century. Buckler produced an impressively accomplished recreation of Westminster Abbey's Lady Chapel, built in 1220–45, which had been demolished in the early sixteenth century.

These mighty rooms are the setting for magnificent collections of pictures and furniture. Realizing that he could never buy medieval furniture in quantity, the Duke acquired considerable quantities of English and European sixteenth-century pieces, which sit happily with furniture brought to Arundel from Worksop Manor after that house was sold in 1838. Exactly a century later, a further influx, of outstanding eighteenth-century furniture, followed the sale and demolition of the family's London home, Norfolk House in St James's Square. In 1959 the 16th Duke, who had succeeded his father in 1917, moved out of Arundel into a new house in the park. On his death in 1975, the dukedom was inherited by his cousin Lord Beaumont, who repaired the castle, intending that it should once again be the family home. After restoring and redecorating the interiors, his eldest son, the Earl of Arundel, moved into the castle with his wife and young family. He succeeded his father as 18th Duke of Norfolk in 2002.

Right: *The dining room, constructed by Buckler in the 1890s in the shell of the castle's twelfth-century chapel. It preserves its original electric-light fittings, installed in 1898.*

Below: *The picture gallery, which links the main rooms on the south front, was added in the early eighteenth century and remodelled by Buckler in Gothic form. In the foreground is a pier table designed by G. B. Borra in 1750 for Norfolk House, London.*

FURTHER READING

Mark Girouard's *The Victorian Country House* (2nd edition, 1979) is unlikely to be replaced as the most authoritative and wide-ranging account of the subject. On the issue of house planning it is supplemented by Jill Franklin's *The Gentleman's Country House and Its Plan* (1981). Robert Kerr's *The Gentleman's House* was reprinted with an introduction by J. Mordaunt Crook in 1972 and a complete English translation of Hermann Muthesius's *Das Englische Haus* appeared in 2007. For a good social history of the English country house in this period, see Jessica Gerard's *Country House Life: Family and Servants 1815–1914* (1994). Most general accounts of Victorian architecture offer some account of country houses; the best is Roger Dixon and Stefan Muthesius's *Victorian Architecture* (1978), which includes a dictionary of architects. There is also a great deal of useful information on country houses in Charles L. Eastlake's *A History of the Gothic Revival* (1872); a new, enlarged edition, with an introduction by J. Mordaunt Crook, was published in 1970 (second edition, 1978).

The history of English landed estates in the Victorian era is dealt with most fully in F. M. L. Thompson's *English Landed Society in the Nineteenth Century* (1963); the decline of the political and social value of land is one of the themes of David Cannadine's *The Decline and Fall of the English Aristocracy* (1990). Although it comments only briefly on country houses, Martin J. Wiener's *English Culture and the Decline of the Industrial Spirit 1850–1980* (1981) prompted a major historiographical debate about the relationship between country houses and the nation's industrial and commercial elite. For a full review of this subject, see F. M. L. Thompson's *Gentrification and the Enterprise Culture: Britain 1780–1980* (2001), which contains a great deal of valuable information for a study of Victorian country houses. Professor Wiener has returned to the subject in his introduction to a new edition of his book (2004). On houses built by 'new money', see J. Mordaunt Crook's *The Rise of the Nouveaux Riches* (1999).

The most important monographs on individual architects and designers relevant to a study of the country houses discussed in this book are: Megan Aldrich, ed., *The Craces: Royal Decorators 1786–1899* (1990); Jill Allibone, *Anthony Salvin: Pioneer of Gothic Revival Architecture* (1987) and *George Devey Architect 1820–1886* (1991); David Cole, *The Work of Sir Gilbert Scott* (1980); J. Mordaunt Crook, *William Burges and the High Victorian Dream* (1981); Colin Cunningham and Prudence Waterhouse, *Alfred Waterhouse 1830–1905: Biography of a Practice* (1992); Winefride de L'Hôpital, *Westminster Cathedral and Its Architect* (on J. F. Bentley, two vols., 1919); Rosemary Hill, *God's Architect: Pugin and the Building of Romantic Britain* (2007); Edward Hubbard, *The Work of John Douglas* (1991); Sheila Kirk, *Philip Webb: Pioneer of the Arts & Crafts Movement* (2005); Godfrey Rubens, *W. R. Lethaby: His Life and Work, 1857–1931* (1986); Andrew Saint, *Richard Norman Shaw* (1976); and Paul Thompson, *William Butterfield* (1971). There is still no modern book on Charles Barry, but the 1867 biography by his son, Alfred Barry, *The Life and Works of Sir Charles Barry RA, FRS*, was reprinted in 1972.

LIST OF ARTICLES

The following is a list of *Country Life* articles for which the photographs published in this book were taken. I have given the author's and (in parentheses) photographer's names, where known. I have added other published source material that I drew on while writing the text.

Alnwick Castle, Northumberland: Christopher Hussey, June 22, 29, July 6, 13, 1929 (A. E. Henson); Giles Worsley, December 1, 1988 (Alex Starkey).

Arundel Castle, Sussex: John Martin Robinson, May 23, 30, 1991 (June Buck); John Martin Robinson, April 23, 1998 (June Buck).

John Martin Robinson, *Arundel Castle: A Short History and Guide* (1994).

Avon Tyrell, Hampshire: Lawrence Weaver, June 11, 1910.

Bishops Court, Devon: Chris Brooks, February 15, 1990 (Tim Imrie); Clive Wainwright (on the furniture), October 18, 1990 (Tim Imrie).

Brodsworth Hall, Yorkshire: Mark Girouard, October 3, 10, 1963 (Jonathan M. Gibson); Michael Hall, June 29, 1995.

Cardiff Castle, Glamorganshire: Mark Girouard, April 6, 13, 20, 1961 (Alex Starkey); Michael Hall, December 5, 1996 (Simon Upton).

Carlton Towers, Yorkshire: Mark Girouard, January 26, February 2, 9, 1967; Clive Wainwright, December 1, 1994 (Simon Upton); Michael Hall, February 23, 1995 (Simon Upton).

John Martin Robinson, *Carlton Towers* (guidebook), 1991.

The Chanter's House, Devon: Michael Hall, January 10, 1991 (Tim Imrie).

Cragside, Northumberland: Mark Girouard, December 18, 25, 1969 (Jonathan M. Gibson and Alex Starkey).

Andrew Saint and Sheila Pettit, *Cragside* (guidebook), 1981.

Eaton Hall, Cheshire: John Leyland, August 21, 1897; Anon., April 21, 1901; H. Avray Tipping, May 29, 1920; Clive Aslet (on the estate buildings), March 5, 1987 (Mark Fiennes).

The archive also contains a set of photographs taken by Arthur Gill in 1932 that appears never to have been published in the magazine.

Flintham Hall, Nottinghamshire: John Cornforth, December 20, 27, 1979 and January 3, 1980 (Alex Starkey).

Harlaxton Manor, Lincolnshire: Christopher Hussey, April 11, 18, 1957 (A. E. Henson).

Tim Knox, 'A Palace for an "English Country Squire": Early Designs for Harlaxton Manor, Lincolnshire', *Architectural History*, 36 (1993), pp.94–102.

Hewell Grange, Worcestershire: Anon., December 6, 1902; Anon., August 15, 1903; Michael Hall, October 7, 1993 (June Buck).

Highclere Castle, Hampshire: Mark Girouard, June 18, August 13, 1959; Clive Aslet, June 30, 1988 (Mark Fiennes).

Longleat, Wiltshire: Megan Aldrich, December 7, 1989 (Julian Nieman).

Madresfield, Worcestershire: Anon., March 30, 1907; Clive Aslet, October 16, 23, 30, 1980 (Jonathan M. Gibson).

Milton Ernest, Bedfordshire: Mark Girouard, October 23, 1969 (Alex Starkey).

Old Place, Lindfield, Sussex: Anon., July 20, 1901; Anon., May 23, 1903; Anon., September 21, 1907.

Sandon Hall, Staffordshire: Clive Aslet and Michael Hall, June 13, 1991 (Mark Fiennes).

Paul Bradley, 'William Burn and the Design (and Re-Design) of Sandon Hall, Staffordshire', in *The 1840s: The Victorian Society Studies in Victorian Architecture and Design*, vol. 1 (2008), pp.30–41.

Scarisbrick Hall, Lancashire: Mark Girouard, March 13, 20, 1958; Rosemary Hill, August 8, 15, 2002 (Paul Barker).

Shrubland Park, Suffolk: Christopher Hussey, September 24, November 19, 26, 1953 (A. E. Henson).

Standen, Sussex: Lawrence Weaver, May 7, 1910; Mark Girouard, February 26, March 5, 1970 (Alex Starkey).

Stokesay Court, Shropshire: Anon., December 8, 1900; Anon., February 20, 1904; Michael Hall, August 18, 25, 1994 (Tim Imrie-Tait).

Thoresby Hall, Nottinghamshire: Clive Aslet, June 29, July 5, August 2, 1979 (Alex Starkey).

Tyntesfield, Somerset: Anon., May 17, 1902; Michael Hall, April 18, 26, 2002 (Paul Barker).

James Miller, *Fertile Fortune: the Story of Tyntesfield* (2003)

Waddesdon Manor, Buckinghamshire: Anon., December 20, 1902.

For a bibliography of Waddesdon Manor, see Michael Hall, *Waddesdon Manor: The Heritage of a Rothschild House* (2nd ed., 2009).

Wrest Park, Bedfordshire: Anon., July 9, 16, 1904; Simon Houfe, June 25, July 2, 1970 (Jonathan M. Gibson).

Wood House, Essex: Mark Girouard, December 31, 1959.

INDEX

Page numbers in italic refer to photographs or captions